"Extraordinary . . . reinvents the role of writing as the ultimate catalyst for creative thinking and practical problem solving."

—Tom Peters

"Brilliant, absolutely brilliant. Most people think with their mouths when they should be thinking with their fingers. Chapter 7, 'Go with the Thought,' is alone worth the entire price of Mark Levy's remarkable new book."

—Al Ries, coauthor of such bestsellers as
Positioning, The 11 Immutable Laws Of Internet Branding,
and The 22 Immutable Laws of Marketing

"I am a great believer in the power of writing to shape a corporate culture, and to sharpen one's own mind. I was delighted, then, to read Mark Levy's **Accidental Genius**, which teaches readers how to use writing to get more out of their thinking than they ever thought possible. I am certain any businessperson could profit mightily from reading—and using—this book."

—Alan C. Greenberg
Chairman of the Board
Bear, Stearns & Co., Inc.

"**Accidental Genius** ought to be required reading in all our schools. Mark Levy ought to be appointed Guru of the Library of Congress. I've always believed everybody has a genius locked up within them, but Mark shows how to give wings and words to that genius. His book is the most extraordinary I've read on the real art of writing, which means the real art of opening up your mind and letting your real self and your best ideas come out on paper."

—Jay Conrad Levinson, author of the
bestselling Guerrilla Marketing *series of books*

"Businesspeople owe Mark Levy a wild round of applause for **Accidental Genius**. From its lively voice to its practical wisdom, this book teaches us how to be great while being patient with our imperfections."

—Lynn Kearney
Director, the Write Effect, and Professor,
New York University's Stern School of Business

"Mark Levy is right on about writing; he understands implicitly how the non-conscious thought process expresses itself through the written word. There is real insight in this book."

—Roger C. Schank
Director, Institute for the Learning Sciences
at Northwestern University, and Chairman
and Chief Technology Officer, Cognitive Arts Corporation

"Energy jumps from every page, invigorating the reader with a dynamic, powerful approach to problem-solving."

—*Michael J. Gelb, author of,* How to Think Like Leonardo da Vinci: 7 Steps to Genius Every Day

"There's nothing accidental about the genius of Mark Levy's techniques for stimulating the thinking process. His inspiring ideas have endless, practical application for the busy business person."

—*Ron Bauer, author of* FOS: Forget Operating Systems, *and other* "Eye-Openers"

"This work expands one's understanding of how thinking works."

—*Ray Peterson*
Director, The Institute for Writing & Thinking
Bard College

"Talk about big ideas in small packages! This slender book reveals the very alchemy of how to think creatively. The ideas in **Accidental Genius** are ridiculously strong and useable."

—*Paul Harris*
Director, The Institute for Advanced Astonishment,
and named by Magic Magazine *"One of the*
100 Most Influential Magicians of the Century"

"Use this book to unleash the power of your own writing NOW!"

—*Bob Nelson*
President, Nelson Motivation Inc., and author of 18 books, including the
million-copy bestseller 1001 Ways to Reward Employees

"Levy's eye-opening book isn't really about writing—it's about thinking. In its striking, funny, jarring way, his advice shook the cobwebs off of my thinking patterns and made my daily confrontation with the word processor something to look forward to."

—*David Pogue*
author of 15 books, including the bestseller
Macs for Dummies

"Mark Levy has rendered his passion, perfectly, onto the pages of **Accidental Genius**. His fire will help you find your own fire. It is essential that you read this book."

—*Cliff Hakim, author of* We Are All Self-Employed *and*
President, Rethinking Work®

Accidental
GENIUS

"The act of writing stimulates thought,
so when you cannot think of anything to write,
start writing anyway."

Barbara Fine Clouse
Working it Out: A Troubleshooting Guide for Writers

Accidental GENIUS

Revolutionize Your Thinking Through Private Writing

MARK LEVY

BK

BERRETT-KOEHLER PUBLISHERS, INC.
San Francisco

Berrett-Koehler Publishers, Inc.
450 Sansome Street, Suite 1200
San Francisco, CA 94111-3320
Tel: 415-288-0260   Fax: 415-362-2512
Website: www.bkpub.com

Ordering Information

Individual sales. Berrett-Koehler publications are available through most bookstores. They can also be ordered direct from Berrett-Koehler Publishers by calling, toll-free; 800-929-2929; fax 802-864-7626.

Quantity sales. Special discounts are available on quantity purchases by corporations, associations, and others. For details, contact the "Special Sales Department" at the Berrett-Koehler address above.

Orders for college textbook/course adoption use. Please contact Berrett-Koehler Publishers toll-free; 800-929-2929; fax 802-864-7626.

Orders by U.S. trade bookstores and wholesalers. Please contact Publishers Group West, 1700 Fourth Street, Berkeley, CA 94710; 510-528-1444; 1-800-788-3123; fax 510-528-9555.

Printed in the United States of America

Printed on acid-free and recycled paper that is composed of 85 percent recycled waste, including 10 percent postconsumer waste.

Library of Congress Cataloging-in-Publication Data
Levy, Mark. 1962–
    Accidental genius : revolutionize your thinking through private writing /
by Mark Levy.—1st ed.
        p.   cm.
    Includes bibliographical references and index.
    ISBN 1-57675-083-3
    1. English language—Rhetoric—Problems, exercises, etc.   2. Critical thinking—
Problems, exercises, etc.   3. Business writing—Problems, exercises, etc.   I. Title
    PE 1479.B87L48   2000
    808'.042—dc21   00-031157

First Edition

03 02 01 00   10 9 8 7 6 5 4 3 2 1

Designed by Detta Penna

Contents

Foreword

After thousands of years' worth of writing about writing, including Strunk and White's modern classic, *The Elements of Style*, could there be anything left to say on the subject? Before reading Mark Levy's *Accidental Genius*, I would have said no. But now? Yes!

Yes, a dozen times over!

This, simply, is an extraordinary book. It re-invents the role of writing as the ultimate catalyst for creative thinking and practical problem solving.

Levy, at an early juncture in the book, describes a magic trick that falsely purports to demonstrate mind reading. Well, the joke is on him: He read my mind! This book, in addition to teaching me a dozen new lessons, confirmed—and made clear for the first time—my own approach to writing, and how I've used it—freestyle—to help me stay ahead of the fast-paced game in which I participate.

As you can tell, I love this book. It is magical! And, ultimately, timely. Why the latter?

This is an era in which economic value—witness Microsoft and the Web startups—derives almost entirely from inspired head work, not heavy lifting. Any of us who wish to survive economically must be good communicators . . . and must constantly and creatively add new value by re-inventing ourselves. This book makes a genuine and wholly original contribution towards those ends. It is not a "must read." It is more a "MUST ABSORB AND LEARN FROM."

Way to go, Mark Levy!

Tom Peters
West Tinmouth, Vermont

Preface

What do you think these are?

-

-

-

-

Measles? Poppy seeds? A row of buttons?

No, they're bullet points—empty bullet points.

You don't often see empty bullet points, because a bullet point by its very nature is only supposed to appear if it's pinning an interesting idea to the page.

But it's my contention that more bullet points should remain empty, and more memos should remain unwritten . . . at least until the businesspeople who write them put some *original thought* into what they have to say.

Now this notion of original thought isn't as ominous as it sounds. When I say businesspeople should give their subject original thought, I don't mean they should grit their teeth, ball up their fists, and squeeze until a trickle of insight runs off their brow. Heck, no!

Instead, I'm saying they should have fun with their subject. Give it fresh attention. View it from different angles. Pursue it through changes in context.

Why the mind games?

Because even the most tired subject has its intrigue, even the toughest problem has its solution, even the most obscured opportunity becomes evident, when studied from enough unconventional perspectives.

That's what this book teaches: *It helps its reader use writing as a world-examiner and perspective-twister for greater success in business and in life.*

Or, as they'd put it in a continuing education catalog:

LEARN HOW TO

THINK SMARTER

Do a Better Job

ACHIEVE YOUR
HIGHEST ASPIRATIONS

VANQUISH YOUR FOES

and Double Your Joy

for Life

Through the Magic
of Private,
Playful Writing!!!

Interested, so far? Good. Here, then, is some more preface-like information that you might like to know, after which, we'll roll up our sleeves and get to work.

Who should read this book? You, of course. Why do I say that? Here's my ingratiating, though honest, answer:

Although we've never met, I already know a thing or two about you: You're bright and ambitious. How do I know?

You've picked up a book that promises to help you use writing to make a difference in the world. Believe me, no dim, lethargic Joe or Jane Q. Public is going to even consider reading a book like this. And if you were assigned *Accidental Genius* as part of a course, then your teacher thinks of you as someone bright enough to handle this type of material.

But what if you only think of yourself as bright in certain situations? That's normal. In fact, none of us is continually bright.

And although none of us continually has our brinpower switche don "High," we're all capable of producing bursts of exceptional insight, or what might be called *genius moments*.

Genius moments usually come to us as something of a surprise, at those times when our minds force unexpected connections between ideas, or consider a problem from a striking perspective. In the grip of such moments, we become our own experts, our own best counselors.

So how might you go about generating genius moments? The most important thing is to forge they exist. That's right, forget about your smarts, your wisdom, your genius. Put all your effort into stretching your thoughts, and into the mechanics of freestyle writing (which you'll learn about soon).

Must you be a good writer to achieve results with this book? No. As a matter of fact, if your writing is forever elegant and readable, you're hindering your best thinking.

After reading this book, will you increase your ability to produce memos, reports, and books? The qualitative thinking you put into these works will increase by leaps and bounds. You'll delight yourself with vivid demonstrations of your own natural genius *(and believe me, even if you already think of yourself as brilliant, you've got smarts that you haven't even touched yet)*.

Who am I? I'm a guy who has used writing to make a difference in my job and my life.

For the past fifteen years, I've worked in the wholesale, retail, and publishing segments of the book industry. During that time, I've sold over a quarter of a billion dollars worth of books, have been nominated for three prestigious "Rep of the Year" awards, and have spearheaded projects that involved some of the business world's most sought-after stars. All these accomplishments were made possible, in part, through my informal, exploratory writing.

I've also used the type of writing you'll be reading about to help me write books and advertisements, as well as articles for prominent newspapers.

Are all the techniques in the book field-tested? Absolutely. In fact, the ideas in here have a glorious lineage. Scientists, like Charles Darwin, writers, like W.B. Yeats, and businesspeople, like Tom Peters, have used these strategies long before I ever learned them.

What, then, is my original contribution to the material? This: Whereas most of these luminaries have used the techniques in this book to improve their *writing*, I have used them as a practical way of focusing on *business achievement*. That's what you'll learn: mind-popping methods of bringing your own genius to bear on business achievement.

So keep a pen and notebook close at hand, or power up your computer. In a few moments, you'll be writing. We have important work to do.

PART ONE

Your Bankable Head

1

Thoughts as Currency

In addition to my work in business and as a writer, I also perform magic tricks.

In fact, I perform a particular trick that bewilders people; some audiences even get the idea that they're witnessing "the real thing." Here's what happens:

I ask a gentleman volunteer to *think* of a single playing card, while a lady volunteer stands opposite him, doodling on a pad. "Draw whatever you like," I tell her, "a scene from a dream, a word, a detail from your day."

I then tell the audience the following:

"Tonight, I'm going to show you how easy it is to read minds.

"Reading the mind of another person is no big deal. There's nothing mystical or metaphysical about it. All you have to do is exploit certain scientific principles that operate with everyone.

"First, you need to exploit the principle that thoughts have an actual weight and spatial dimension to them."

I offer proof for my claim by citing an old *Scientific American* article about brainwave-measuring machines. "So if you can measure a thought," I reason, "it obviously has mass to it." I continue:

"Second, you need to exploit the principle that thoughts actually jump from our minds all the time, like electricity does when it completes a circuit. That explains why, at times, a strange thought will suddenly appear in your head for no apparent reason. Chances are, you got in the way of someone else's circuit-jumping thought, only you didn't realize it."

At this point, I dramatically stop the doodling lady, and ask her to hold the pad up high for all to see.

There—impossibly—hidden among the rough imagery of her doodle, is the very name of the gentleman's imagined card! The lady, it seems, has read the gentleman's mind.

Amid the audience's gasps, I say, "Amazing, isn't it? Science at work."

Of course, the magician's code forbids me from divulging how the trick's done, but that's not the point. The point is this: I've presented this trick to shrewd corporate vice-presidents and street-savvy entrepreneurs who bought its pseudo-scientific premise because it seemed so plausible, they said, *given the times we're living in.* Here's what they mean:

We're living in a time where companies are making Godzilla-sized fortunes without inventories, buildings, or even workers. *Hard assets are out, invisible assets are in. Ideas rule the business day.*

Companies worth millions—Millions? Hell, billions!—are somehow leveraging their smarts, their imaginations, and are ringing registers worldwide by bringing their head-built products to market.

Take Microsoft, for instance. Here's a company with $1.5 billion in hard assets, yet it has a market value of over $318 billion. That means the "invisibles" of the company—"goodwill," perceived brand value, and the thoughts percolating in Bill Gates' noggin—are worth three hundred times the company's "touchables."

No wonder my stories about weighty, jumping thoughts have a ring of truth to them.

We live in a world where thoughts are a potent, industry-driving currency, where major corporations set up complex systems for managing "Intellectual Capital" and "Information Technology" just so they can mine and protect the valuable thoughts of their workers.

This is dizzying, large-scale stuff—and it's hard to appreciate on a personal level, even if we're involved with one of these fast-moving, knowledge-worker companies ourselves. But whether we can fully comprehend this grand revolution or not, we can draw a helpful, human-sized conclusion from it, and that conclusion is this:

The ideas and observations careening around like lottery balls inside your mind have a real-world value to them—if you can get to them, develop them, create with them, make them practical.

That, then, is what this book is about: *it teaches you how to get at what you're thinking, so you can convert the raw material of your thoughts into something useable, even extraordinary.*

How do I propose to help you get to these extraordinary ideas of yours? Through writing. Or, more specifically, through something called *private writing.*

Private writing—a phrase coined by two brilliant writing teachers, Peter Elbow and Pat Belanoff—is a fast, for-your-eyes-only method of thinking onto paper that enables you to reach a level of thinking that's often difficult to attain during the course of a normal business day. By exploiting a few secrets, you'll delight yourself by happening upon ideas and know-how you may not have realized you possess.

And what are these secrets? Here they are, in bare bones form:

- Don't show your private writing to anyone (this essential secret powers all the others in *Accidental Genius.* I'll explain why throughout the book.)

- Allow yourself to think badly and write poorly (chapter 3)

- Write as quickly and continuously as your hand can move (chapter 4)

- Attack a situation for a prescribed period, and then move on to other things (chapter 5)

- Tap your most honest ideas by using "kitchen language" and jumps in logic (chapter 6)

- Extend your thoughts beyond their normal bounds (chapter 7)

- Redirect your focus, often (chapter 8).

Hanging out there like salami on hooks, these secrets might not seem the most nutritious food to feed your revolutionary mind . . . but wait. As I make my case for these "salami," and as you put them into practice through your writing, you'll wow yourself with what you discover—and apply to your life.

Points to Remember

- Every recognized innovation has, in some way, been a product of human thought. It stands to reason, then, that the thoughts appearing in your mind have an enormous potential value to you and the world.

- Sometimes your best thoughts must be coaxed out, and played with, before they reach their fullest potential.

- The world's most progressive companies have sophisticated infrastructures just to develop, and protect, the kinds of thoughts that you've already had or are capable of having.

2

What to Think About

Before we examine private writing's brain-pumping secrets in detail, you might benefit from knowing when your writing skills will benefit you.

Try your hand at a few minutes' private writing if, for instance, you're...

- brainstorming ways to stay close to your customer

- building an interactive website

- driving an advertising campaign in an intriguing direction

- deliberating about who to partner with

- fantasizing about how to spend your bonus

- revisiting vital points from a meeting

- explaining tax laws to yourself

- debating whether to fire an assistant

- fine-tuning plans for the building of a community center

- charting the course of the planets

- turning an observation into a poem

- crafting your poem into a ballad

- musing about how to explain sex to your child

- choosing between a white or a burgundy interior for your new car

In other words, there's nothing too small or large, abstract or concrete, ordinary or unusual for you to write-and-think about. The world is a spinning mass of fertile material for you, and whatever puts a glimmer in your eye, a bounce in your step, or a curse upon your lips is what you should write about.

But let's say those examples aren't enough. Let's say you understand that you can write about anything and everything, only you're not fired up about it. It's too big a concept to wrap your mind around. You need a smaller target, something with a finer focus. Enter Tom Peters.

You know Tom Peters, don't you? He's the man who the phrase "Business Guru" was invented for, the man who taught baby boomers that they could and should do work that was simultaneously important and fun.

During one of his lectern-pounding, insight-flinging seminars, Peters offered up the following advice—advice which can easily and productively be appropriated in your hunt for absorbing things to write about: *"Get a notebook,"* he said, *"write 'Cool' on the front, and 'Crappy' on the back, and fill it with cool and crappy stuff."*

That is, use a notebook as a kind of treasure chest, or junk drawer, into which you toss loose observations and curious facts—and dip into it whenever you feel the need.

By using the galvanizing poles of "cool" and "crappy," you'll find yourself awash with material to write about. Why? Everybody loves and everybody hates. It's easy to fill in those blanks.

Points to Remember

- In private writing, if you can think about it, you can write about it.

- Sometimes, answers to Big Problems only come once we've mulled over small problems.

- Fill a notebook with "Cool and Crappy" observations. That way, you'll always have ideas to use, problems to solve, and raw material to fill your head.

PART TWO

The Six Secrets to Private Writing

3

Secret #1: Try Easy

Robert Kriegel, business consultant and "mental coach" for world class athletes, tells a story in one of his books that has critical implications for you in your quest to lead a better life through writing.

Kriegel was training a sizable group of sprinters who were battling for the last spots in the Olympic trials. During a practice run, Kriegel found his runners to be "tense and tight"—victims, apparently, of "a bad case of the Gotta's."

Conventional wisdom would have dictated that these highly-skilled athletes train harder, but Kriegel had another idea. He asked them to run again, only this time they were to relax their efforts, and run with about nine-tenths their normal intensity. Of this second attempt, Kriegel writes:

> "The results were amazing! To everyone's surprise, each ran faster the second time, when they were trying 'easy.' And one runner's time set an unofficial world record."

Fine for running, but does that idea hold for any pursuit? Kreigel continues:

"The same is true elsewhere: trying easy will help you in any area of your life. Conventional Wisdom tells us we have to have no less than 110 percent to keep ahead. Yet conversely, I have found that giving 90 percent is usually more effective."

For private writing, too, Kreigel's "easy" notion hits the nail on its relaxed head.

Rather than approach your writing with your teeth gritted, demanding instant, virtuoso solutions from yourself, take a chill pill, and ease into your best 90 percent effort. Here's how:

Begin your writing by reminding yourself to "try easy." I liken this to the prep work of a baseball player upon stepping into the batter's box. The player adjusts his batting glove and cup, spits, kicks at the dirt, stares at the barrel of his bat, and eases into a few practice swings. These rituals accomplish two things: they allow the hitter to set up the "mechanics" of his swing, and they get him in the correct frame of mind to face a pitch.

That's what I'm asking you to do. Get your mechanics down, then do a psych job on yourself. Or, put another way: *Start scribbling, then remind yourself that you're simply looking to put some decent words and ideas down on the page—you're not trying to produce deathless prose and world-beating ideas in the course of a single night's writing.*

I've opened my computer's private writing file to find a few examples of how I remind myself to "try easy." I don't have to look far.

Nearly every entry begins with a reminder, invocation, plea, entreaty, or some declaration of assurance from me to myself to stay centered during the writing, and not expect wisdom, insight, or shining prose. Most of the time, I don't specifically say to myself, "Try easy," although the sentiment is there. Here are some samples:

Remove the "Mighty Specialness" of writing, until there's nothing to stop you. This kind of writing is dirt simple, like putting on a sock.

Just some brain-draining, some noodling, going on here. Don't expect lightning bolts.

Okay, a little sticking here to start, like a computer key that hasn't been deep struck for a while. Keep moving and the stickiness may or may not leave, but at least you'll be moving.

Here it is, on the line. I'm squeezing some words onto the page, but I'm scaring myself with demands of originality. If words don't come out of me in interesting arrangements, tasty strings, then my writing fingers slow down, my mind stops. Wait, Mark. That kind of thinking is going to guarantee you no new ideas. Better just forge ahead, and get some stuff onto the page— great or stink-o.

Hardly inspiring openings, I grant you. But if you, like me, suffer from wanting to accomplish too much, right away, an honest attempt to calm your expectations can improve the quality of your thinking in the long run.

You, though, might be wondering, will all this self-reassurance act as an anchor on my thinking, and weigh it down far below what is helpful? Might I, in effect, be courting my own dumbness, inviting it into my home in the same way an unsuspecting damsel invites in a vampire by thinking him a charming stranger?

The answer is no. Despite your pleas and cautious self-instruction, your mind still begs to solve problems and do extraordinary work. By giving yourself this "try easy" ground rule, you'll ease up on your perfectionistic demands, and give your rampaging mind more room to maneuver.

But wait, I have another way—a way virtually guaranteed to move you into that try easy zone....

Points to Remember

- A relaxed 90% is more efficient than a vein-bulging 100% effort.

- When you begin your private writing about a thorny subject, remind yourself to "try easy."

4

Secret #2: Write Fast and Continuously

That's right: when you write fast and continuously, you pretty much have to adopt an easy, accepting attitude—you don't have much choice.

My assertion, though—that fast, continuous writing improves thought by relaxing you—needs clarification: Just how fast? Just how continuous?

First, just how fast? I'd say about as fast as your hand moves when you scribble a note to your best office buddy, saying: "Couldn't wait for you anymore, went to lunch at Giuseppe's," because your colleagues were already piling into a car, and you wanted to get a seat next to that good-looking new hire, so you could offer up a steady line of witty asides on the way to the restaurant. You know, fast.

By going fast, you invite your mind to operate at a pace that's closer to its normal rate of thought, rather than the lethargic crawl you usually subject it to when you write sluggishly.

Here's what I mean, crafted into an experiment: In your mind, summon up the image of something that happened to you yesterday—a

SUBJECT...

freedom. If can't really do anything faster than I normally do. I'm engaging in nothing. No hurry. Keep writing. This isn't to me working. I need a focus, a genie ready to rock. Tom Weller Being a credible teacher is part boasting. Don't be afraid to boast but put enough effort into what you're doing so that people remember what you want them to remember. What is it about you that's stopping you from giving this some real thought? A fault in you. Overuse

RECYCLED PAPER

When you do private writing, don't fool yourself into thinking you need a fancy diary in which to record your thoughts. A co-opted piece of paper will help you do the job just fine. And if what you've written seems unimportant, chuck the paper.

much better you fewel knowing you've excelled. Look at the incident with Jorge yesterday. He didn't get his books, told you not to worry, and hung up. That wasn't good enough for you. You stayed on top of the problem util it was solved. (of course, you must call UPS Monday morning). But you felt confident that you did what you were supposed to do. You operated on principles. You didn't consult a manual or suddenly read a book on how to satisfy the customer. You followed some internal guidance system that smart, creative, responsible people like you have. How many people would have gone to those lengths? Few. It wasn't a BZ problem. But you instinctively knew ht handle it. IN THE SAME WAY, YOU INSTICINTIVELY KNOW HT WRITE HT PUT DOWN IDEAS IN A FRESH VIOICE, HT TELL WHAT HAPPENED IN A WAY THAT RECREATES THE EXPERIENCE FR THE LISTENER, EVEN IF YOU ONLY USE A FEW WORDS TO DO IT. SO THAT'S A GOOD START IN RECREATING MY JOB. I NEED TOP FLESH OUT THIS BUSINESS BOOK ASPECT MORE SO THAT IT DOESN;T FIZZLE, YET NOT FORGET THAT I HAVE A DAILY SALES ASPECT TO IT TO. LET'S LOOK AT THAT FIORST:

I HAD THE IDEA OF GOING PAST THE FIRST ORDER GIVER SO THAT WHEN THAT PERSON LEAVES, I'M SYTILL HELD IN GOOD STEAD. I NEED TO RECORD THE GOOD THINGS I DO FOR ACCOUNTS SO THAT WHEN THEY CHANGE PITCHERS, I CAN BACK UP WHAT I'VE DONE WITH FACTS (I MADE CERTAIN YOU GOT YOUR BOOKS NEXT DAY. IO GAVE YOU X WHEN NO ONE HAD IT.) DO THAT ON YOUR POWERBOOK PROGRAM. OBVIOUSLY, YOU NEED A SCREEN FOR EACH ACCOUNT, AND IT WON'T JUST HAPPEN NATURALLY. YOU'LL HAVE TO STOP, ACCESS THE ACCOUNT, AND TYPE IN THE INFO. KEEP TREACK. ALSO, WHEN YOU PUNCH UP THAT ACCOUNT, YOU'LL HAVE NOTES TO WORK FROM THIS TIME WHEN YOU TALK WITH THEM. PROBLEMS? YEAH, PUNCHING THE ACCOUNT UP ON BZS COMPUTER AND THE MAC AT THE SAME TIME. WAYS AROUND THAT? CAN I HOOK THENM UP TOGETHER? CAN I GET A DUEL SCREEN PROGRAM ON THE BZ COMPUTER THAT WILL RECORD INFO WHILE I'M TAKI[NG THE ORDER? Hey I did ll this in caps. Actually, I like the look of urgency in it when I looked up. Accidents yield results, good, bad, neutral, interesting. Bing. What else? When I'm on this duel screen (fictional at this ounching) I might have to send an order before I've written everything down. PerhAps this screen could hAve the last order date and amount on it. Perhaps I can access it after I've sent the order, just so I can put my notes ionto it.

That's worth developing, looking further into it and flipping through the available programs to see what can be used off the shelf and custom jmade (Good project for me Steve and Pogue). What though right now (continue to look ahead though, don't denegrate what doesn't yet exist. Just what can I do given what I have at this moment?) I can have the Mac open at the side left right in front of me part of my desk and enter before after during my conversations. Check out the programs in the house now. I can put together a provisional list of who I'll call today, including the order and the phone numbers. I can custom make my book list within my computer, Including quotes I want to use and key words.

When you do private writing on a computer, experiment with typography as a means of shaking up your thinking. Also, print out your work and pick through it with a pen so you'll remember points you want to expand upon in later writing.

meeting with the boss, a decision you made about the market, etc. Take pen and paper, and start to write about that image, but write slowly, perhaps at half your normal speed. Spend a few seconds on each word, as your hand traces out the line and curve of each letter. Keep this slowness going for two minutes.

Difficult, huh? Did you find, in a sense, that your mind followed your body, that your thinking slowed down to accommodate the snail's pace of your hand? It's almost as if your mind were saying, "Why should I give that situation a good thinking through, if my hand isn't going to have time to record what I'm pondering. Nuts to this." Your mind then either slowed down to match your hand speed, or it wandered off and distracted itself in trivia.

Now do the opposite. Conjure up the image, but use the next two minutes to get it down on paper twice as fast as you normally would. You needn't push yourself towards bionic speed—just move as quickly as you can without cramping your hand. *Try for, say, forty words in a minute.* If you want to vary your speed, by all means do, but don't drop back too far. And if you want to talk to yourself on the paper as you're speeding ("This feels interesting, but awkward"), go ahead and talk.

How was that for a difference? Forget about the quality of words, and just look at the product of your labor. You've doubtless used ten times the amount of ink, gotten further in your story, and accomplished a bit more advanced thinking than you did at slow speed. You may not have done anything that seems impressive yet, but you've demonstrated to yourself, in a small way, that there's a radically different level of thinking going on when you write at a speed closer to the speed of thought.

On to the second question: Just how continuous? I'd say about as continuous as your grip on the report you spent weeks preparing, only to find out that you didn't address the issue most dear to your CEO. You know, continuous.

By writing continuously, you force the edit-crazy part of your mind into a subordinate position, so the idea-producing part can keep up production by spitting out words.

What I just wrote is true, but somehow, the rich ideas bundled up in that lone sentence need more room to breathe. I guess I figure that if your attention inadvertently lagged eight seconds back—maybe your toddler plopped her spaghetti dish on her head like a hat, or a passing car blared its radio—you'd miss one of the most critical conceptual statements in the book. Here, then, is that same sentence, with its root ideas unbundled, expanded, restated, and dressed up in smart-looking bullet points:

- If your mind knows your hand won't stop moving, it'll ease up on trying to edit out your "inappropriate" and underdeveloped thoughts.

Normally, your controlling mind censors you because it wants you to look good to yourself, and to the public. Now, though, it knows it's been backed into an impossible position; it can't possibly examine your quickly-appearing thoughts for public-correctness, so it recedes into the background.

- *Your "inappropriate" thoughts are "where the action is," and the more quickly you get to them, the more effectively you can fashion solutions for yourself.*

What are "inappropriate" thoughts? Bone-honest notions you wouldn't normally air in public. Things like, "I hate my payables department," and "Just for kicks, I wonder what kind of products we would have to invent if we junked our cash-cow?" These thoughts, in large part, contain your genius.

- Your continuous writing acts, in a sense, like a brainstorming session with yourself, but in many ways it's better than traditional brainstorming.

While traditional brainstorming asks you to withhold judgment on spontaneously-voiced ideas, we all know that's impossible. In public, you can *curb* your judgment a bit, but never completely suspend it. In your private writing, however—since no one but you will see it, and your edit-crazy mind is napping—you can access your wildest associations without fear of reprisal.

- Because you have to come up with something to say while you're writing continuously, you stay focused on what you're writing, knowing that if you lose your place, you'll have to stop, double back, and pick up the thread of your logic—thus breaking your self-made promise to write continuously. Your normal writing approach doesn't have this Zen-like, stay-in-the-moment focus.

- Continuous writing shows you that individual thoughts are cheap, since you always have new ones following on the heels of current ones.

But what if you have to stop because you've run out of things to say?

Write meaningless stuff while waiting for your mind to redirect you. That's right—vacuous, senseless, meaningless stuff.

Babble onto the page: "I went to the hen for twice times two phone drake dreg parala..."

Repeat the last word you wrote: "The data show show show show show show ..."

Or the last letter you struck on your keyboard: "The profit I I IIIII-IIIIIII..."

Just keep your writing hand revved up and occupied, while your mind quickly considers its options then gets on to a new thought.

Got it, then? The plan is to move rapidly, and don't stop writing, with the understanding that the more words you pile onto the page, even if they're lousy words, the better your chance at finding a usable idea.

In the private writing game, think quantity before quality. As sci-fi great Ray Bradbury says about story writing: "You will have to write and put away or burn a lot of material before you get comfortable in the medium."

To apply it to private writing, I'd change this quote to read: "Write with a fast, haphazard hand, because you'll need to burn through all the awful stuff you smear onto the page in order to get to something halfway decent." *That's the way to think: the bad brings the good—and there's no way around this natural order.*

Points to Remember

- If you write as quickly as your hand can move, or your fingers can type, and you continue to generate words without stopping, astonishing things will happen. Among them: your mind will eventually give you its Grade A, unadulterated thoughts to put on the paper, because it realizes it won't be criticized (no one but you will see them), and you might be able to use them (thoughts can be tweaked and developed, once they're on paper).

- If you temporarily run out of things to say, keep your mind and hand in motion by repeating the last word, or letter, you wrote. You can also accomplish the same thing by babbling onto the page in a nonsensical, "scat" language.

- Your best thought comes imbedded in chunks of your worst thought. The only way to reliably mine your best thought? Write a lot. Think "quantity." Think "word production." Think of yourself as a word and thought factory.

5

Secret #3:
Work Against a Limit

Let's apply some of the information you've learned so far. Set your kitchen timer to ring in ten minutes and...

What's that? I haven't yet spoken with you about using a kitchen timer as a writing aid? Shame on me. Once you start using a timer to help you generate thoughts, you'll never be without one. Your kitchen timer, in fact, will become the most important item on your desk—with your computer running a close second.

Here, then, is why you need the timer: It provides you with a time limit against which to conduct your thinking. That's critical, for two reasons:

1. *The limit energizes your writing effort by giving you parameters.*

Think of it: If I ask you to write fast and continuously about some emotionally charged difficulty you're having at work, how long do you think you could keep the words flowing? Pondering a tough subject—especially from a variety of angles, as I'll teach you—is both exhilarating ... a nd exhausting. You can't keep going forever, or even for a short—if indeterminate—amount of time.

See, when I'm asking you to write privately, I'm asking you to sprint. Now if I specified that you were to sprint flat out for a short, designated distance—say, forty yards—you'd hoof it. But if I implored you to sprint for a vague range—say, between forty *yards* and forty *miles*—you'd hold down your speed, and wait to see how far you'd have to go. You'd put in a lesser effort because the parameters of the race were uncertain.

A timer—preset for ten, or even fifty minutes—energizes you in your thinking campaign, because it specifically limits the amount of work you have to accomplish in a single bout of writing. Once that timer rings, even if you're in the midst of a sentence, you stop. In a sense, the timer enforces a self-imposed behavioral contract: You promise yourself to think and write deeply for a certain period, you do, and then you can put your feet up.

2. *The limit keeps you writing, so you'll have a chance for a genius moment.*

And then there are "those days." On those days when you're brain-dead, or tired, or uninspired, but a presentation is due and you've got to come up with something, your commitment to your timer will keep you writing. True, most of what you produce during this time will be loathsome, but some of it may be useable, or even better than useable.

In the world of private writing, it's a truism that oftentimes your freshest notions come when you've let your guard down, and you're writing absolute junk. Call it "try easy," or "lowering your expectations," but sometimes your bored, or disgusted, junk-writing mind redirects you toward places your excited mind bypasses; *history is, in fact, full of people who had extraordinary ideas when they were in low, seemingly unproductive, states.*

The keys, then, are to keep working, even when you're covering your page with babble, and to keep writing, until your timer tells you to stop.

That last paragraph would have been a good time to close this chapter, don't you think? If I had quit twenty-odd words back, I would have left you on a high note, with the image of a swiftly-writing-you shining in your mind, as you tried capturing your own genius moments, no matter what the mood you found yourself in.

But if I had stopped there I would have cheated you out of a small, yet significant, detail: Buy yourself a timer that doesn't make a clicking noise as it counts down. No wind-up dial timers, or dimpled, plastic lemons with green numbers running around their circumference that twist in half to activate the timing mechanism. Believe me, you'll thank me for this advice. That clicking noise can be very, very distracting. I thought you should know.

Points to Remember

- Writing for short, timed cycles (normally in the ten to twenty minute range) concentrates the mind.

- You needn't feel chipper to have a world-beating thought.

  Try This: Start with a three-minute writing exercise. Grab your "Cool and Crappy" notebook, and pick out a head-shakingly cool observation. Write about why you think that particular item is cool, using all you've learned so far (try easy; write fast and continuously).

6

Secret #4:
Write the Way
You Think

If you've ever been given advice on how to prepare a document for the business community, you've doubtless been admonished to "Write the way you speak." That is, you've been asked to make your document sound conversational—and, therefore, easier to understand—by using contractions, plain words, personal pronouns, and a dozen mini-rules, which give the impression that you're somehow hovering behind the reader, whispering directly into his ear (although if he were to try and shoo you away, there'd be nothing there for him to swat).

This plain English style of writing is invaluable when you're trying to communicate with others, but of lesser value when brought to the private writing page. It's not that the "write the way you speak" tenets are wrong during private writing, it's that they don't go far enough.

During a bout of private writing, it's imperative that you get at your raw thoughts before the prissy side of your mind cleans them up for public viewing, and, in the process, squelches their effectiveness. I ask you, then, not to "write the way you speak," but to "write the way you *think*." Here's what I mean.

So far, this chapter is composed of the kind of language I use when I speak. True, I've edited out lots of "Umms," "You knows?," and other brain-fart fillers that stink up my spoken messages. But if you and I were to have an in-person conversation, you'd certainly recognize me as the same guy who wrote this text, given my vocal cadence, word choices, and expressed thoughts. To you, this Mark-as-writer and Mark-as-speaker would have congruence, because in both instances I'm using the same part of my brain that dresses up thoughts for public consumption.

When I write for myself, however, I don't necessarily access this publicly oriented part of my brain. *I use the writing solely as a way of watching myself think.* Here's an unedited, honest-to-goodness example of a writing session during which my recording hand merely followed the path laid down by my coffee-soaked brain:

Let's try one with muscle. Lots of useless writing. Abandon the logical edge.

This paper will come up from my gurgling stomach, and I'll burp it across the page. Of course, from bleech to finished product often comes out compromised, a provisional bleech. But this is an experiment.

As Glenn says, the review is short enough to do two, three, four reviews, an entire book of reviews, written by me on the same Ripken book, each expressing a different point, or the same point in different language; here wharf foreman, there dancemaster. So where's the beef, huh? What should I look at?

I tried initially to cull the crunchy details from Iron Man and paste them into some A to B form. To Stella and Susan, that worked. But to Michael and Floyd, it didn't. How can I use good details (there are few to spare), and paste it down to a vivid review, giving Michael 'something I can't forget'?

To you, this passage probably reads like gibberish, despite the fact that the words I use in it are, for the most part, conventional, and the sentence structures that house those words, ordinary. From your perspective, this passage might seem a failure of communication. To me, it's just the opposite.

This passage so clearly mirrors the way thoughts bound around my head, that even today, five years after I wrote it, I can clearly see all the points I was driving at.

I achieved this miraculous clarity through these three techniques:

1. *I used kitchen language.* What the heck is kitchen language? Well, I don't know for sure, since I pulled the term out of an essay by freewriting pioneer Ken Macrorie, and in that particular essay, he didn't define it. But I have a pretty good idea what the term might mean, and for the purposes of this book, let's assume that, son of a gun, I'm correct and my meaning is, in fact, *the* meaning.

Kitchen language, then, is the language you use around the house when you're lounging in knock-around clothes, as the television hums pleasantly in the background, and you yap with your best friend on the phone. It's good, strong language, but not the kind you'd normally use to get your point across in most settings. *Kitchen language is your own slang, the words you use that best capture the idea of a thought or an object, even if you're the only one who "gets" what you mean.*

In the above private writing excerpt, I used the kitcheny "bleech." What does "bleech" mean?

Judging from the language proceeding it—words like "gurgling" and "burp"—I assume that it's a hybrid of "belch" and "retch," and I used it metaphorically, to express the feeling I get when trying to expel ideas during a writing session. "Burp" would have been too weak, "retch" would have been too violent. Therefore, "bleech."

I followed up my kitcheny coinage with the bizarre phrase "provisional bleech." At first glance, that phrase—even given my definition of "bleech"—might appear difficult to dope out. But not to me: Since provisional means "temporary" and bleech "expulsion," I was obviously reminding myself that the creative process is messy, but that the mess is, at once, necessary and temporary.

Could I have used more conventional language to make that point to myself? Of course. But during that particular writing session, my racing mind decided "provisional bleech" was what I needed to say. *I didn't sit at my desk and deliberate about it. I merely followed what my mind asked me to write naturally.* That's what you should do, too.

Just concentrate on writing loosely and honestly about the subject at hand. Strong kitchen language will come instinctively.

2. *I kept quiet about those things that needed no explanation.* Since I was writing for myself, I didn't name all the "characters" involved in the situation, or hack through all the background information surrounding it. If I were writing for others' eyes, of course, I would've had to pencil in some kind of headline, like: "Re: My review for the Times." I would've also had to explain that "Glenn" was a publisher friend of mine who'd read an early draft of my review, etc. But for myself, it was unnecessary.

3. *I jumped around.* When you're writing for other people, you need to develop ideas convincingly, and make certain that your readers are clear about where your narrative is headed. In private writing, however, *by following the mind's natural workings you can drop all pretense to sound argument and the logical connection of material.* I'm not asking you to delude yourself into accepting faulty arguments. I'm only saying that during any given bout of writing, your reasoning need not be airtight. Feel free to jump around as it suits you.

Points to Remember

- Private writing isn't writing, per se; it's a means of watching yourself think.

- Since you're writing for yourself, you needn't spit-shine your raw thoughts to please others. All that matters is that *you* understand your logic, references, word choices, and idiosyncratic ideas.

Try This: Pick another cool observation, and write about it for five minutes, incorporating everything you've learned (if you'd like, scribble the secrets at the top of your page as a cheat sheet).

When your time is up, review the writing. If you can read it aloud so that others fully understand it, you're stifling your most honest thinking. Do another five minutes' writing and try to get your *exact* thoughts on paper.

7

Secret #5:
Go with the Thought

In the mid-1980s, I took an improvisational theater course, hoping to hone what I considered my most bankable gifts—wit and joke cracking. At the time, I fancied myself something of a Woody-Allen-in-training, and I figured an improv course would give me a wide, well-lit platform on which I could show off. Boy, was I mistaken.

The teacher of the course was an old-school improv troupe member, and he frowned upon any attempt by his students to be conspicuously funny on stage. Humor, he preached, must flow naturally from the situation being portrayed, and should never be forced into it by Borscht Belt wannabees.

So class after class, he would toss a few students on stage, yell out our fictional identities ("Mark, you're a homeless person. Cindy, you're a businesswoman on the way to the train"), and give us a scene to act within ("Mark, you try to convince Cindy to give you money").

Begrudgingly, I delivered lines that logically followed my co-player's lines ("Ma'am, do you have fifty cents for a hot meal?"), while I gulped back the absurdist, out-of-left-field dialogue I longed to spew ("Ma'am, I just peed on myself"). When that course ended, I turned my back on improv theater ethics, or so I thought.

Half a dozen years later, while doing some private writing about a troubling business situation, I found myself unexpectedly embracing the improvisational philosophy I had earlier rejected. I wrote:

> *Remember your improv training. You must go with the situation set up for you.*
>
> *If you're taking premise-suggestions from the audience and someone wants you to be a dentist giving a cleaning, for example, that's what you must be. You can't suddenly chuck the scenario in mid-speech, and say, "Oh, you thought I was a dentist, but I'm really a gynecologist, or a shoe salesman, or a kodiak bear." Also, you mustn't contradict the lines fed to you from your fellow actors. If a co-player says, "Dr. Levy, here are those X-rays you wanted," you shouldn't say, "I didn't ask for X-rays." That reply kills the scene. There's nothing to say after that.*
>
> *Instead, if you want the scene to march ahead, you take that X-ray line and create within that context. You pretend to study the X-rays, and say something like: "Look at this, all your teeth are molars ... Look at this, you have no teeth, only cavities ... Look at this, your teeth aren't numbered like they were in the dental school cadaver ... " Stuff like that. Be funny if you like, but within the logic presented.*

In the few moments it took me to compose this writing snippet, I realized that the improv ethic—go with what you're given—wasn't the ponderous, rain-soaked, woolen overcoat I thought it was. Rather, this philosophy liberated the mind by giving it a specific ground zero from where to begin its thinking.

Throughout my subsequent private writings, I referred to this improv strategy again and again, reminding myself to "go with the thought" I had just put onto paper. I felt great energy in my thinking and writing, as my hand raced to keep up with my mind.

The whole time I was scribbling, I would say to myself something like, *"Go with the thought. Agree with what you just wrote, and logically extend it . . . Be whimsical if you like, but make sure the whimsy naturally follows what preceded it... Based on this new thought that has just appeared on the page, what might happen next?"*

This intoxicating game of "agreeing and extending," during which I would effortlessly flesh out scenarios, would take up pages of my writing, until my hand grew tired, my timer went off, or even more important, I had discovered some provisional methods for tackling a problem.

To make this all clearer, let's set up a little learning lab situation for you. Rather than asking you to jump right in and use the concept on a situation from your own life, let's shift the perspective and add some playfulness to it while you learn.

For the next ten minutes, you're not you. You're Jennifer, a marketer for BeefSalami.com, a year-old company that sells salami over the Internet. Given your heavily defined niche, you control ninety percent market share in Web-based salami sales. But your profits aren't where you'd like them to be. What can you do?

To begin (after your "try easy" invocation), you might tell yourself why you're sitting there writing. Something like, "Selling salami on the Internet gives us a defined market niche, but is far too restrictive to enable us to grow," would do.

Then you might ask yourself about the different sides of the business—the product, its marketing, the billing, competitive sites—to see where you'd like to direct your thinking.

Suppose, being a marketer, your attention gravitates towards the public's perception of your product. Most people, you assume, perceive salami as a low-class, school-lunch, nitrite-ridden, amalgamation of cow parts stuffed into an edible membrane casing (you realize, perhaps for the first time, that the cow wasn't born with a specific "salami" organ). How, you wonder, do we change that perception?

What about positioning salami as an upscale product? All right, then, how do you "go with that thought"?

On the paper, you have a starting point—creating an upscale salami—and in your next sentence you take a step that plays off the thought that preceded it. Perhaps, you write, an upscale salami might be wrapped in gold foil. Good. What else? It might come in a dignified wooden box, like cigars. Snob appeal. Great. An upscale salami might have some kind of medal and ribbon attached to its package, signifying what? Quality meat... an award winner... imported from some romantic locale... sanctioned by some prestigious organization. What organization? The government... an existing industry body... a organization BeefSalami.com helped create?

If I go with that last thought, you wonder, where will it lead me? *You have no way of knowing, until you write it down and follow its call:*

BeefSalami.com could chair some kind of appointed committee to assure the public that Web-based meat products would adhere to high standards, higher, even, than those demanded by the U.S. Government. The U.S. Government? Why stop there. Go with the thought . . .

BeefSalami.com could chair an industry-standards organization that makes certain that Internet meats around the world conform to certain health and taste requirements. Around the world? That would give us an international presence. It's true, you write, that by virtue of being on the Net, BeefSalami.com already has an international presence. But by being part of a sanctioning body, the company could form crucial alliances with meat producers from other parts of the globe. We could translate our web page into two dozen other languages and advertise our product in the appropriate countries as an exotic import....

You continue writing down associative thoughts as they come, until you feel you've said what you needed to say. At that point, you stop—or do you?

By all means, halt your private writing if you believe you've ferreted out some good ideas, or you have a better handle on your situation. Remember, though, there are other avenues for you to explore, if you're up to it. *Despite the seemingly inevitable logic by which each thought grew out of its predecessor, someone else might have taken a particular thought in a different direction.*

Let's go back to the beginning of our scenario. You've been thinking about the public's perception of salami, but you want to explore an alternate route: Maybe changing the audience's perception of the meat isn't necessary. Maybe BeefSalami.com could play into the fact that the product is a down-and-dirty meat, a meat of the streets. How would you prove that?

Or maybe your initial premise is wrong. Do you know for sure how the public views salami? How might you gather pertinent information about what people think about your luncheon meat, and how might you use this information when you get it?

Is the tight niche of Internet-salami-seller one your company should continue to work within? Whether it is or not, it's certainly worth a few minutes' time contemplating the thought of how you might expand your focus.

And what of the other numerous approaches? So far, you've been looking at the goal of bigger profits through a marketing and sales lens. But how would you approach it from an accounting or operations perspective? You needn't have perfect knowledge of these fields to poke around in them—at least, not on the private writing page. *A timid first sentence scratched onto the paper, and the ability to tease a next, timid sentence from that first one, will do the trick.*

Okay, let's shed our Jennifer persona, and reinhabit our own form-fitting personalities. To go with a thought in your own writing, it isn't necessary that you choose some vital problem and give it lots of serious, preliminary thought. Just grab a problem, any problem, and write about why it bugs you. Then, as a thought experiment, add a small change to the scene and follow the implications of that change from one scene to the next. If you let your hand move swiftly enough, and you give yourself permission to play, you might just find yourself sporting a fresh idea or two.

Points to Remember

- When you "go with a thought," you assume that a particular thought is true, and you take a graduated series of logical steps based on the thought. ("If A could be true, that means B could be true. And if B could be true, that means C could be true. And if C could be true...").

- Since situations are complex structures, there are many directions you can move around in them, and still be working within the situation's "logic." (For instance, you and I discover that our company's postal meter is broken. If I go with that thought, my logical responses might deal with finding who's to blame for breaking it; your responses might deal with getting the meter fixed.)

Try This: Pick a crappy situation from your notebook, and go with it for five minutes. At the end of five minutes, reset your timer, and go with it in a completely different direction. Be sure you obey all the secrets of private writing during this exercise in "agreeing and extending."

8

Secret #6: Redirect Your Attention with Focus-Changers

With pen in hand or computer powered up, you begin a private writing road trip about something important to you. Perhaps you're thinking about how to announce a fee increase, or you're wondering how best to approach your boss to ask for higher-visibility projects. Whatever the situation, you're on the private writing bus, motoring along, when suddenly you hit the brakes.

The road ahead is washed out, and you don't know how to proceed.

Quickly, you consult your checklist of private writing rules: Try easy, check. Writing fast and continuously, check. Inoffensive kitchen timer counting down ten-minute intervals, check. Now you've run out of ideas. You've reached the end of your thoughts, or so you believe.

While you stare ahead at the washed-out road, a distant light glimmers to your left. Why, there's a highway out there! How could you have missed it?

Then, to your right, a loud honk. By gum, a road leading to a major city! Yet you passed it without noticing.

You look around. Roads, exits, and towns are everywhere, only you failed to see them while your eyes were trained ahead.

I call these roads, exits, and towns "focus-changers," and they're available to you on every private writing road trip.

But what is a focus-changer? Nothing more than a *question you ask yourself on paper, which requires you to comment on something you've just written.*

Not only do I use focus-changers whenever I write privately, but I also use them in public documents. As you comb through *Accidental Genius*, you'll constantly see me asking myself questions like:

- *What was I thinking here?*
- *How else can I say that?*

Those are two of my favorites. They push me to re-see what I've done, and think I already know. They also challenge me into generating fresh thought—even after I believe I've run out of road.

But those aren't the only focus-changers you can use.

Focus-changers have endless numbers or forms. Here's a partial list of some helpful ones:

- *How can I make this exciting?*
- *How can I add value?*
- *What else can I say about this subject?*
- *Why am I stuck at this particular point?*
- *How can I get unstuck?*
- *What am I missing here?*
- *What am I wrong about here?*
- *Why?*
- *How can I prove that?*
- *How can I disprove that?*
- *What do I think about that?*
- *What line of thinking led me to that conclusion?*

- *If I continue to think that way, what might happen?*
- *What other problems like this one have I experienced?*
- *What solutions can I borrow from past problems that can be applied to this current one?*
- *What does this remind me of?*
- *What's the best case scenario?*
- *What's the worst case scenario?*
- *What am I doing right?*
- *What am I doing brilliantly?*
- *How can I jump the track?*
- *Which strengths of mine (or my company's) can I apply?*
- *Which weaknesses need to be compensated for?*
- *Where's the proof that that statement is true?*
- *How am I the wrong person for this project?*
- *How am I the right person for this project?*
- *How would an arbitrator judge that?*
- *If I wanted to make a big mistake here, what would I do?*
- *What data do I need that I don't yet have?*
- *How can I better use the data I already have?*
- *How would I describe it to the CEO?*
- *How would I describe the situation to my mother?*
- *How would I describe it to my most supportive friend?*
- *How would I describe it to a disinterested stranger?*

You get the message. When you've come face-to-face with a stumper, a puzzler, a bewilderer, use one of these to start a new conversation with yourself. Or invent your own.

What you might also do: Reread the list of focus-changers and check off the two or three that most intrigue you. Copy those favored focus-changers onto a scrap of paper and keep it next to you during a private write. When you hit a wall, or just for giggles, grab one and see where it leads you.

Points to Remember

- Focus-changers are simple questions to ask yourself, in writing, which help you re-direct your mind towards the unexplored parts of a situation.

  Try This: Reread one of your writing pieces, and note where a focus-changing question would have led you in a different direction. Do ten minutes' private writing on this new direction. If you start to run dry of ideas before the ten minutes are up, use other focus-changers to revitalize your thinking.

Part Three

Powerful Refinements

9

Idea as Product

Writing teachers often tell students that "writing is thinking." They say this to de-mystify writing and to wipe away the students' anticipatory tension in putting pen to paper. These reassuring teachers believe that if you can think clearly, and use the language of daily speech, you can express yourself competently on the page.

This is valuable advice. The more we think of writing as nothing special, the more we think of it as just another way of expressing ourselves (like speaking to a friend over the phone), the better off we are.

But for those of us trying to use our writing to solve problems, the logical question is, why write at all? If "writing is thinking," why not dispense with the writing altogether and get down to some hard thinking? Two reasons, I believe, underline the importance of getting your ideas down on paper, of making them a touchable product.

First, the physical act of moving your pen across the page, or hitting computer keys, is a powerful focusing force.

Human thought, by nature, bounces all over the place; that's why most prolonged bouts of serious thinking degenerate into daydreaming.

Suppose I'm managing some service workers who have a problem communicating with each other in front of customers. These workers normally get into pointless debates about procedure, confuse one another, and end up arguing.

If I try to think my way out of this situation, I may get some strong ideas. But just as likely, my thinking will edge towards tangential affairs, until I forget why I initiated my mental problem-solving campaign.

I'll picture the workers in the situation, particularly the trouble-maker, Mike. Then I'll remember that Mike owns a Jeep Cherokee like mine. That'll remind me to take my Jeep to Jiffy Express to get the oil changed. I take it there because their staff shout out the oil-changing actions they take ("Changing the filter!"), and these cries have an impressive, military efficiency to them. I also like the fact that the boss, Russ, knows me and gives me a discount and. . . .

My good problem solving ideas dissipate, evaporating somewhere between the catalyzing problem and my drive over to Jiffy Express. That, in my experience, is how the human mind works.

There's nothing wrong or unusual about this mental divergence and far-flung association. In this situation, though, I didn't use my mind's natural workings to reach a productive end. That's a trap of thinking without a physical object to focus one's attention.

When you write and create a product as you go, it's a simple matter to bring your attention back to the subject at hand. No swami-like mind control or puritanical discipline is needed. Even as you diverge from your main subject, the fact that you're sitting and scribbling jars you into remembering that you started your writing efforts with a specific purpose.

There's a story about Thomas Edison that relates to this. Edison would rest in his chair while holding a handful of coins, so when he lapsed into sleep, the coins would fall, hit the floor, and wake him—a cacophonous reminder to get back to work.

The physical act of writing is your handful of coins. Let the divergences in your mind come, write about them if you wish, but as your divergence winds down, wake yourself into realizing that you had a starting point which still needs attention.

The second reason why you should create a written record of your thinking is that it leaves you with a bread crumb path down which you can retrace your steps. This point is similar to the first one, but with several important distinctions.

In any given bout of private writing, the drifts your mind takes can hold your richest thinking. It would be a shame if these potentially fertile drifts were lost to you because you couldn't recall them. Most people lose the power of these drifts, however, because they trust their memory when they shouldn't.

In one workshop setting, for instance, I informally interviewed students about their jobs for twenty minutes at a time, and wrote down key identifying words as they spoke (without letting them see what I was writing), so that I could accurately recall their talks—main subject and digressions.

I then asked each student to revisit what they said, and repeat all the points they could remember. On average, these students remembered only half of what they had told me only moments earlier.

I am asking you, then, to write out your quickly passing thoughts as if they were gold, because some of these thoughts may be of incaluable value to you when examined at the proper time.

Look back to the earlier "customer service/Jiffy Express" scenario as an example. I first introduced that anecdote as an example of unproductive daydreaming. My goal was to think up, without committing to paper, a few ideas to solve an important, reoccurring work problem. But my good intentions drifted off towards getting my Jeep serviced.

If this same digression played out on paper, though, with a chance to redirect attention and review some tangential ideas on the page, I might have gotten a possible solution out of the situation.

While writing about the Jiffy Express, I might have paid more attention to the military shout-out method their staff uses to service a car. Perhaps such a verbal checklist could be applied to the customer service problem my employees were having? Maybe, maybe not. What's important to note here is how my private writing acted as a bullpen to hold the digressions in check, so they could be studied for their associative power.

Points to Remember

The conversion of your thoughts into a paper product is important for these reasons: It . . .

- keeps *unproductive* daydreaming to a minimum.

- allows you to hold your main idea at the forefront of your mind.

- permits you to follow your associative line of thinking back to its origin.

- gives you something solid from which to criticize, and create.

- enables you to study your thinking from one day to the next.

Now you may be thinking "Wait a minute. This is no recap. Mark didn't overtly discuss all these points in this chapter." That's true. What I did do was reread what I had written, what was staring at me in black and white off the page, and allow the writing to suggest this new point, which I acted on:

- Just as your written product shows you where you've been, it also suggests where you haven't been.

  Try This: Write about a problem situation for five minutes, and put it aside. Now, in a second five-minute session, try recalling all the details and digressions you made during the first five minutes. What did you leave out the second time? What did you inadvertently add?

10

Open Up Words

Here's a page from my private writing file:

> *I yawn when I see an author use the word "empowerment."*
> *Sure, I understand that the word is supposed to mean "decentralization," and "giving everyone, including the front-line worker, power to make decisions that help the customer." But unless the writer is someone I trust, someone I know who has thought about the word 124 times and put it into practice himself, I think most writers use the word because it sounds high-minded.*
>
> *The majority of the business world doesn't use empowerment as a practice, at least, not effectively. For most business people, empowerment is an untested concept, or a rationalization for a disinterested, laissez faire management style.*
>
> *Here are more problems inherent in the conventional idea of "'empowerment." If workers are truly empowered, they're going to make mistakes, probably in front of the customer. Sounds good in a business book, but not so good when a lengthening line of exasperated customers roll their eyes in front of you . . .*
>
> *If workers are truly empowered, they may use their autonomy as a way to justify laziness, explaining away their inefficient*

service as something they thought was necessary, given the situation…

If workers are truly empowered, they still need monitoring because they're executing actions out of the accepting norm, actions which may have untold, company-wide ramifications.

I know I'm playing the stinker in this writing. Someone sees what I just wrote and thinks I'm a strict, follow-the-rules, hierarchy guy. Which I'm not. I vehemently believe in empowerment, at times. I do, though, have enough mistrust of people not to hand them the keys to the organizational kingdom just because it seems like the enlightened thing to do.

After eyeing the above excerpt, you're probably settling back in your chair and thinking, "Okay, a chapter on the evils of empowerment. How is Levy going to drive home his point, I wonder?" But no, I've pretty much said all I have to say about empowerment, at least in this book. The subject of my excerpt takes a back seat to the method I had in mind while I was generating it. This private writing excerpt was produced while I engaged in a technique I call "open up words."

When you "open up a word," you re-define that word (or the phrase that contains it) so it has personal meaning. You, in a sense, become an explorer within the word, forsaking the sleepy meaning others have given it, and discover for yourself if the concepts embedded within it are still valid. Like a medical student who learns to heal by dissecting a cadaver from head to toe, you strip off the word's skin and unravel its guts, to study its fundamental premises. Here's how I go about it:

1. *Pick a word to examine.* As you comb through a management text, a magazine article, or your private writing, or as you work your way through a business day, you'll come across words whose definitions seem taken for granted, words which are used as a way to stop thinking, rather than start it. These are the words to pay attention to.

Perhaps you'll happen upon a term, like "empowerment," which people uncritically accept as goodness incarnate. That's a word to set aside for study.

Perhaps you'll discover a term, like "budget cut," which instantly brings on sour stomach. Words in this camp also deserve a closer look.

Perhaps, too, you'll run into a term, like "industry," whose meaning seems neutral. These words often yield the grandest surprises when deconstructed through your writing.

2. *Give yourself a common definition of the word.* If you look back to my empowerment excerpt, you'll see that I begin by laying bare the word for what it really is, including its most overused, lifeless connotations. I tell myself what other people "see" when they discover the word on a page or come upon it in life.

3. *Ask yourself if you agree, or disagree, with the common definition, and explain your choice.* Because you've already put down a base definition on the page, you have written thoughts to build upon.

4. *Ask yourself what kind of thoughts and images you may have the next time you come across the word.* After slogging through people's dead language, playing with your own insights, and arguing up a storm, your equilibrium may be thrown off if you don't summarize where you've been and what you've learned. Tell yourself, in a simple paragraph or two, how you've strengthened your "knowing" through opening up the word.

Let's put all I've mentioned together, and see how "open up words" operates in practice.

From my bookshelves, I've drawn a volume, *Expanding Our Now* by Harrison Owen, in which I'd previously underlined this paragraph:

"Management would have you believe that there is a procedure for every necessary activity, and of course work must be done according to the procedure. But the reality is rather different. More than occasionally it is necessary to 'work around' the procedures to get something done. Work-arounds are treated a exceptions, but I strongly suspect work-arounds are the rule." (pp. 69-70)

Certainly, these sentences are without "fog," or an ounce of obscurifying fat. But without opening up that phrase, "work-arounds," we may forget the concept by the time our eyes have skipped on to the next paragraph. Here's how you might give that phrase a deeper reading through private writing:

'Work-around' is Owen's expression for doing things not-by-the-book, in order to get results. That phrase sounds right to me, but why?

For the most part, I believe we perform certain tasks today because people before us performed those tasks. If different people preceded us, we'd today perform different tasks.

It's kinda like a "What would have happened if..." speculation story, where, say, the Nazis won World War II. If they had won, I probably wouldn't be sitting here typing on my laptop about this subject. Instead, I may never have existed. Or I'd have existed and died. Or I'd be doing something perhaps far removed from what I'm doing now.

Same thing with regards to the goals we value and the way we go about obtaining those goals.

I value literature, but that's because there was a literature system in place when I arrived in this life. If the people before me hadn't valued literature so highly, and, instead, found great personal expression in, say, collecting leaves, maybe my goal today would be leaf collection. I don't think I'm that creative or iconoclastic that I would have pioneered the field of literature by myself. I wouldn't have thought about the written word, and if I did, I probably would have thought it trivial.

This idea of those-before-us-set-ground-work-for-the-way-we-operate-today holds in smaller ways, too.

When my lawn is overgrown, I either fire up the mower or

call a service. But I do those things because I was taught to do them, overtly or through a kind of lawn care osmosis. If the hordes of people before me hadn't thought that tending to lawns was important, I'm sure I wouldn't be doing it today. If those pre-me people never had lawns, I'm pretty certain I'd never have one.

Okay, Levy, ground yourself. How does all this talk of Nazis and lawn care relate to the phrase, "work-arounds"?

This way: "work-around" sounds like when you do it, you're doing something wrong. It sounds like, "Sure you're getting the job done, but you're being unnecessarily show-offy and difficult in order to do it—a cheater, not a team-player." Actually, though, when you (appropriately) "work-around" you show that you understand that most processes are jerry-rigged—that is, there's nothing sacred about them, they're just there to accomplish a goal. If other unused, or unthought-of, processes help you better get the job done, then use those.

How have I worked-around recently? Oh, yes…by helping a bookstore client of mine get books for their author signing.

A prominent author was coming that night to do an announced signing, and the store discovered they didn't have enough copies of the author's book for her to autograph.

Now my involvement should have conventionally stopped when I told the store's book buyer that I couldn't get him copies in time for the event. But I worked-around this standard answer with some divergent thinking, and by overstepping what would normally be considered my boundaries.

I gave the buyer a bunch of options that he'd never heard of before, but seemed reasonable to me: call the author and see if she has stock she'd bring; call her publisher and see if they could jet over stock; if the normal channels at the publisher were stock-poor, make sure to check with the author's editor, who might have sample copies lying around; ask to borrow copies from friendly, surrounding stores; buy copies from rival

surrounding stores to save face (I'd place the calls, if he liked);
offer to ship the book for free, and affix and autographed sticker
inside it, when the stock did arrive...

Through a combination of these strategies, everyone came
away from the signing happy. This story may not have the power
of my Nazi-victory scenario, but it works for me. I demonstrated
this concept of work-around, by using every unconventional
method I could think of to get my customer books, even if my
involvement overstepped what a wholesaler rep should do.

So with all I've just written, what should I take away with me
about "work-around"? If you truly want a result, don't worship
the conventional route that most people follow to get the result.
That route was probably invented through trial-and-error, and
if different trials-and-errors had been attempted, you'd have a
different route to take today.

Before we finish here, note this intriguing point: I began the chapter by opening up "empowerment," and finding the concept lacking. I finished the chapter, however, by opening "work-around," and found it invigorating. What's the similarity and difference between the two? Perhaps you'd like to write about it.

Points to Remember

- To open up a word, write down four things: a word for study; the generally agreed-upon definition of that word; your thoughts on the accuracy of the definition; and a personal definition that suits your eccentric tastes.

- In private writing, always explain to yourself why you think what you think. Often, you'll realize you have no basis for your belief. What then? Apply a little mental elbow grease, and come up with a belief that will better serve you.

  Try This: Make a list of five common jargon words in your industry, and open up each for five minutes.

11

Get Unreal with Reality-Tweaking

In chapter 7, "Go with the Thought," I told you how to follow an idea until it reached its logical conclusion. Now I want to add rocket boosters to that technique.

Here, then, is a valuable new way to go with a thought, a way that I first read about in the work of cognitive scientist, and mega-genius, Roger Schank. Let's call this whimsical technique "reality-tweaking."

To tweak reality, *radically* alter one detail of the situation you're studying, then go with it, and "discover" how your radical alteration plays out, exponentially changing the entire situation.

Suppose you're a computer consultant, and you're having a tough time prospecting for clients while servicing your current ones.

During the course of three nights' writing, you've dumped a lot of facts and opinions into your private writing file. You feel as if you have a clear understanding of the situation, but you're no closer to a solution.

A particular aspect feels important to you, though: Your current clients love the fact that you give them extra work for free during the course of a project. They look upon your unbilled hours as their much-deserved "value-added extra" for hiring you.

This is the spot in your writing where you try a capricious, fiction-based, reality-tweaking experiment.

Instead of giving your clients these extra hours for free, you charge for them. Not just any rate. A jumbo rate. Two, three, even 1000 times your normal fee. That's your reality-tweaking starting point.

Now go with that mutant thought. Based on this fantasy starting point, how would everything in the situation change, particularly as it relates to your prospecting efforts?

For one thing, your clients would value your normal hours more than they usually do. Since overtime might cost them hundreds of thousands of dollars, they'd have all their supporting work done and waiting for your expertise, because they wouldn't want you to hit "golden time." And since you wouldn't be putting in extra time, you'd have your nights free to plan and execute your marketing campaign.

Of course, if you did reach overtime, you'd make so much money that you could afford to let your prospecting lapse, at least for a while.

What else might happen because of your exorbitant charges? Companies would think of your service as more valuable to them, in order to justify their expenditure on you.

And? They'd pay you a generous retainer's fee, so you wouldn't bring your brilliance to their competitors.

And and? The major financial magazines and television shows would pick up on your story, and do profiles on your monetary wizardry. You wouldn't, at that point, need to prospect since you'd be turning away thousands of multi-nationals demanding your service.

And and and? You could lower your normal hourly rate, since your overtime rate and retainer turned you into a tycoon.

Or, you could take the opposite approach, and raise your normal rate, while lowering your overtime.

Or, you could lower both your rates, and save on taxes.

Or, you could become classified as a national treasure.

Or, you could ask for payment in plutonium…

While you investigated these ridiculous, yet intriguing scenarios, you'd no doubt be smiling and unclogging some pathways in your mind that had been blocked from shooting too low.

Sure, in one sense, this kind of writing seems to be a time-waster, since these fantastic scenarios probably won't happen. But in another, very real sense, you'd be gaining time, by quickly creating the raw material that your more practical side could cobble into a doable solution.

Think of this reality-tweaking heuristic as the "extreme" version of "go with the thought." If "go with the thought" is skiing, reality-tweaking is double black-diamond skiing, on one leg, with no poles. Twist stuff around. Alter things in radical ways. Get unreal.

If an element in your situation is...

- small, think of it as tiny or jumbo

- tall, think of it as sixty stories high or sub-basement

- red, think of it as black or paisley

- time-sensitive, think of it as past-its-due-date or needs-to-be-finished-in-fifty-years

- important, think of it as critical or trite

- thin, think of it as withered or obese

- clever, think of it as genius or dopey

- velvet, think of it as rose petals or canvas

- an expense, think of it as an investment or a step towards bankruptcy

- loud, think of it as an air horn blast or a whisper

- a nuisance, think of it as intolerable or a blessing

- abnormal, think of it as freakish or natural

- crowded, think of it as bulging or empty

- funny, think of it as side-splitting or grave

- wet, think of it as soggy or tumbleweed dry

Remember, you can always work your way back to "reality" from fantasy. Without consciously playing with fantasy, however, you may never realize the potential that awaits you. Viva indirection!

Points to Remember

- Under the guise of being "realistic," we often limit ourselves more than we need to and choke off our chance to a genius moment. One way out of this trap is to use fantasy consciously in our private writing, as a way of testing alternate universes and ways of acting.

- When you play the reality-tweaking game, you pick out an arbitrary spot in a situation to "go with" until all realism falls apart. Later, you can sift back over what you've scribbled for flecks of valuable thought.

  Try This: Pick out a cool observation from your notebook, and write about it for ten minutes, paying particular attention to its most curious feature. In the course of your writing, go with this feature, making it more pronounced, and examine how the rest of your cool observation changes because of your tweaking.

12

Hold a Paper Conversation

Me: *My problem, lately, is that when I meet with resistance from a sales prospect, I get taken aback. See, I've done this job for so many years, and have made my accounts so much money, that I assume everyone should trust me implicitly and instantly see the enormous value in dealing with me. I know that's the wrong way to feel, but it happens.*

David: *Actually, there are at least two reasons why there's nothing wrong with feeling that way. First, as you know through experience, feelings just happen—sometimes for no traceable reason—so it's unnecessary to hold yourself responsible for having a specific feeling. Second, if you really have helped many customers over the years, then these prospects probably would benefit in dealing with you—only they might not be aware of that.*

The only problem I see would be if you let your feelings adversely affect your behavior when dealing with these prospects. If you, for instance, speak harshly to them or don't follow through on what you say you'll do.

Me: *Right. That's a good way of looking at it.*

David: *A realistic way, yes.*

Me: *Let me see if I understand this: As long as I want new accounts, I'm going to meet people who don't know me or my reputation. My job, then, is to accept my feelings as they are, while I try to educate these potential accounts, through word and deed, about why they should deal with me.*

David: *Yes.*

Now, that conversation with David Reynolds—a prominent practitioner of Zen-based, Japanese therapies—helped me immeasurably. In it, David reminded me to do what was under my power to control, and leave the uncontrollable alone. But there's something else you should know about that conversation: it never happened.

David, to be sure, does exist, and I've had a dozen enlightening conversations with him, but this one I made up during a private writing session. Why?

Because I had a workplace problem that needed a little study, and I thought my paper version of David could help me examine it in a productive way.

I could have just have easily summoned up Andy Grove, Susan B. Anthony, or my local grocer, and have received different counsel. The choice was mine to make, and easy to carry out, given the freedom of the private writing page.

Having conversations with others in your writing is most certainly a make-believe game—I, after all, couldn't know for certain how David Reynolds would answer me, unless I actually spoke with him—but it's a perspective-and-indirection-powered game that offers the private writer genuine benefits.

Genuine benefits? How?

Here's one example: Lynn Kearney, a business writing consultant, told me about an executive she was coaching who once used imaginary dialogues in his writing to boost company salaries dramatically.

The exec, it seems, held several weeks of make-believe conversations in a notebook, so he'd be able to go before a board of directors—including the venerable Alan Greenspan—and make a case for pay increases. By the time the actual meeting came around, the exec had answers for every objection the board raised. He went into the situation confident—and came out with hefty bonuses for his employees.

So, holding a paper conversation can help you rehearse how you'd handle a tough situation, "lock in" knowledge you already have, and explore a topic with someone who has already "been there."

Holding a paper conversation also gives you the advantages of speaking with a good bartender: You feel listened to, and you learn things about yourself and your situation, even while the bartender's only contribution to the talk is putting coasters and napkins in front of you.

Who should you speak with? Dialoguing with a variety of folk, in a host of far-out ways, makes for a paradigm-smashing experience:

- Hold a paper conversation with a co-worker who's giving you problems because he's acting like a jerk. Find out why he's acting like a jerk.

- Converse with a co-worker who has successfully handled a project you're currently tackling. Discover how she did it.

- Discuss a dear topic with someone who holds a view wildly different from your own. Try understanding their position, add to it, and then knock it down.

- Speak to a fictional person who has a combination of thoughts and behaviors drawn from other real personalities.

- Talk to yourself, not as you are today, but as you were seventeen years ago.

- Talk to a future you.

- Remove yourself entirely from the conversation, and encourage a discussion between others (Lao Tzu and a dope; your accountant and Madonna; Bill Gates and a talking dog).

Now, while holding these imaginary dialogues can be a profitable exercise, it's not an easy thing to do. For years, I read self-help books whose authors implored me to set up my own spiritual board of directors and staff it with candidates of superhuman integrity and wisdom, with whom I could converse. The idea was that I could discuss things with the people I most admired, albeit in a fabricated form.

Usually, however, after seating an imaginary Abraham Lincoln, I drew a blank on who else to draft, so all my other boardroom chairs went empty.

There I'd sit, face to face with the president, rarely having the nerve to ask him my petty, simple-minded questions about career and life. At those times when I did muster the courage to speak, Lincoln's replies sounded suspiciously like the replies I'd make, spoken in my own voice.

In fact, anytime I saw a book that asked me to speak with my own fantasy advisors, or, worse yet, walked me through a guided visualization during which a person, animal, or vapor would deliver profound answers to my questions, I tossed the time-wasting volume to my dogs, who gratefully pulled it apart.

What, then, caused me to change my mind about the wisdom to be garnered from imaginary conversations? My forays into private writing.

In my writing, I realized that these well-meaning authors who preached speaking to fantasized prophets had, perhaps, the right idea, but missed the reality-boat in several important ways:

- They asked me to think about my questions, without asking me to write about them. My mind, therefore, wafted about and never returned with anything useable.

- They asked me to speak with someone demonstrably wiser than I, thus scaring me into an uncreative silence. In fact, I felt guilty and disappointed because I wasn't creating anything brilliant enough for my brilliant guides to say.

- They asked me to speak to my guide in an abstract sort of way, without first fleshing my guide out as a person. Subsequently, I'd be addressing an abstraction instead of a vivid image. Abstractions give lousy answers.

- They didn't want me to have a conversation with my imaginary advisor, as much as they wanted me to listen to the insights he delivered. This stance gave me a passive attitude to the exercise.

Through my writing, I discovered ways to make the troublesome exercise actually sing. In particular, I came up with two "rules" to govern my attempts at speaking with imaginary, paper counselors:

Rule #1: Put meat on the characters before making them speak.

Rule #2: Get the characters to make you speak.

Let's examine these rules, one at a time:

Put meat on the characters before making them speak. As I alluded to previously, I have an almost obstinate inability to get my mind around an abstract concept. In school, a subject like advanced mathematics dizzied me, because I couldn't hold its ideas in my hands ("Show me a 'function,' teacher. Where is it in our classroom?"). Same thing with conjuring up people. To converse with a person—even one I'm partially inventing—I need to see them and understand what they've done.

If I asked you to hold an imaginary conversation with Abraham Lincoln, you'd probably hem and haw and mumble a few things about liberty. If I asked you to do two minutes of private writing about him first, you'd probably have a slightly more fleshy portrait of the man, perhaps invoking the Civil War or the Gettysburg Address. If I gave you fifteen minutes, however, and asked you to write more deeply about the man, and asked you to concretely picture the way he looked, and ponder the situations he worked within, you'd have quite a different conversation.

Suddenly, you might picture the weave of his long black coat, the pitch of his brow, his gnarled beard. You might hear his high, squeaky voice, and smell the musky odor of the horse he'd been riding. You'd question him about the war, and why Americans shot Americans.

If your mind digressed, and you followed the digression, perhaps you'd remember your childhood trip to Washington, D.C., where you saw the Lincoln Memorial. You'd tell Lincoln about the trip, and ask him how he felt about his memorial and about the current state of his causes. However the conversation progressed, I'm sure you'd feel you understood Lincoln a lot better than when your thoughts of him stopped at the five dollar bill.

At that point, too, you'd be better able to introduce your modern day problems to him, or your fleshed-out conception of him, and hope for an interesting, perspective-changing dialogue.

What you should do, then, is engage in a bit of Method acting as you hold a conversation during your private writing. That is, *experience being in the presence of the person you're speaking to, and experience yourself as that person. Remind yourself, through your writing, to know what they might know, and act as they might act.*

This character-inhabiting isn't as unusual an activity as it sounds. Many novelists create dossiers about their characters, full of information that doesn't even make it into their novels. These writers, though, don't consider their attention to detail a waste of time, because they figure the more they know their characters, the more interestingly those characters will act.

How far should you go with this? It's all fantasy, so go as far as you'd like. If you know any vocal, or bodily, mannerisms that your character possesses, use them. If they "Ummm" a lot, make them "Ummm" on the page. If they clap their hands when they're excited, listen for sound.

Where, too, is your conversation taking place? On the phone? In person? Is Lincoln joining you for dinner? Fine, what is he having ("Would you like a Perrier, Mr. President?")? Are you taking a walk with him? Good, what's the scenery like ("That's an airport, Mr. President")? Try, in fact, talking to your character in their normal locale

(Lincoln in the White House), and in a spot you'd never associate him with (Lincoln on a roller coaster). Perhaps meet the person over a course of private writings and note where they offer you their best advice.

Get the characters to make you speak. If you're growing uneasy as to the degree of fantasy I'm asking you to entertain, this rule should calm you. It, by all means, also asks you to imagine a conversation with an imaginary friend, but more clearly recognizes the make-believe component of the exercise.

Holding a paper conversation is, after all, a sham. It's a way of getting you to examine your situation through "the mind" of a consultant, astronaut, dancer, etc. Whatever advice you get during the exercise was actually generated by you, no matter how surprising that is. The fantasy element is effective insomuch as it helps you get to the best parts of your mind. This "Get the characters to make you speak" rule acknowledges this, admits your mental strength, and asks your imaginary companion to act merely as a sounding board for you.

Here's another way of saying what I just said: Do the preliminary character-building writing I suggested in rule #1, but *after you've clearly seen your companion, let yourself do the majority of the talking during your chat.* Your companion acts as a kind of paper-Socrates to your knowing-student mind, drawing fresh observations from your own lips. Example:

Me: *Mr. Edison, I'm having trouble completing this assignment. What do you suggest I do?*

Thomas Edison: *How many hours a day do you spend at it?*

Me: *During the week, two hours in the morning, before I have to leave for work. By the time I get home at night, it's eight o'clock or so. I eat dinner, watch a little television, walk the dogs, and go to bed. I do little productive work at night, in general. On the weekends, though, I work on my project, on and off, all day long.*

Edison: *How late into the evening on the weekend?*

Me: *If I'm juiced up with coffee, twelve o'clock.*

Edison: *So on the weekend, you can work well into the evening.*

Me: *Yes.*

Edison: *But not during the week?*

Me: *No, not normally.*

Edison: *Why should the weekday evening be different than the weekend evening? Time is time. A Monday moment at nine p.m. lasts for as long as a Saturday nine p.m. moment does.*

Me: *During the week, I find it hard to concentrate at night, knowing I have to get up for work so early in the morning. I also don't drink coffee late in the day on weekdays, so I'll be able to fall asleep more easily.*

Edison: *Sounds to me like you have a set philosophy of daily workload—one you've decided on through your own calculations, and not one that suits the projects at hand. The human body and mind, if given interesting things to attend to, has much greater stamina than you may think. Do you think this fair of me to say? . . . .*

Notice how Edison is a definite presence in the conversation, has a point of view, and listens to me, but directs my thinking through questioning my ideas, rather than bricking me in behind his own views. This strategy of largely confining your companion's role to that of question-asker keeps you from falling into the trap of expecting too much from your companion and allows you to answer your own questions.

Points to Remember

- When you hold a paper conversation, you engage in a make-believe discussion with someone and get their viewpoint on your situation.

- To hold a powerful paper discussion, you need to do two things: (1) Put meat on the character (vividly experience them in front of you), and (2) Get the character to make you speak (respond to the character's brief answers and open-ended questions).

Try this: Decide upon an opportunity you'd like to investigate (changing departments, creating a new product, writing a book in your chosen field, etc.), and hold a ten-minute, private writing conversation with a paper advisor.

Now, pick out some interesting point from that conversation, and use it as a starting point for ten more minutes' writing with a different advisor.

Continue this find-a-key-point/conjure-up-a-new-advisor/do-ten-more-minutes-of-writing cycle, at least twice more.

13

Drop Your Mind on Paper

Think of private writing as a system of components.

Today you'll take thirty minutes to dump all the information you have about a subject onto the paper, and leave it at that.

Tomorrow, you'll review your info dump and use ten minutes to write out some best-case, worst-case scenarios that stem from your previous day's efforts (more on this in the next chapter).

The next day, you'll decide you want to take your accumulated thoughts and free associate from them for fifteen minutes, allowing the material itself to suggest new avenues to walk.

You're not pleased with your effort, so you try something else: Perhaps a session in which you "open up words" and "hold a paper conversation" for twenty minutes each.

Ah, that's better. Here, among the detritus you've scattered onto the paper, are a couple of fair ideas worthy of further exploration. For some reason, though, you don't do any writing for the next three days.

Then it happens. While you're in the office listening to an on-hold version of "Eleanor Rigby," a light bulb goes on over your head. You grab a pencil stub and a crumpled envelope and write yourself into a useable solution in forty seconds' time—*a solution that, by the way, is a* total rejection of all the ideas you had previously, but which needed the fertilizer of those rejected ideas to flower. In practice, that's the way private writing works. Dirty and effective.

But some people thrive from a more structured approach to private writing. They sit down regularly to write and channel their genius through a codified series of steps.

If that approach appeals to you, get your timer and your writing instruments, because we're about to deconstruct one of your problems with rigorous, scientific efficiency.

Ready?

Okay, set your kitchen timer for, say, twenty minutes, and start it.

In effect, you're going to take your mind and drop it onto the page in front of you. That is, begin to talk to yourself on the paper (or computer), *starting from "try easy," and continuing on to the point in your situation which has the greatest "energy" for you, or where you feel most bugged.*

Forget about making your sentences interesting. Your ideas needn't flow sequentially. Don't bother with correct grammar. And if you spell poorly, that's perfectly okay.

Start explaining to yourself why you're writing about your particular situation, and do it using the same language you'd use in speaking to a smart, concerned friend who really wants to hear what you have to say.

Perhaps you might say something like,

> *I'm sitting here, stupidly pounding these keys, because I've run out of good ideas on how to get more business out of the Amalgamated Pulley Corporation. They used to be my best account, but since they put in Amy as head of purchasing I can't even get my calls returned.*

Or maybe you might begin,

> *I said I'd do Mark a favor by trying out this writing approach, but this seems a bit nutty. Oh, well, since I told him I'd do it, let me tell myself about that portfolio situation which has me a bit confused. It seems . . . .*

If you feel resistance to addressing the situation, or this approach, write about it. Perhaps you want to curse. Perhaps you want to speak with yourself logically. Approach the situation from whatever perspective you choose.

Do this for five minutes, or longer if necessary, getting the facts, and your reactions, down as fast as you can write. *If you suddenly find yourself "dry" of words, talking to yourself on the paper about your dryness* ("Hmm, what else can I say? Have I said it all? That's not possible. This problem's been bugging me so badly that I must think other things about it that I'm not telling. What are they? Oh, yes...."). *Eventually bring your mind back to your troublesome situation,* even if you have to mutter to yourself about information that you already put down on the page.

Now, without more than a brief glance back, write about the part of your situation that *works*. What's happening within it that you like? Are there people within the situation who are doing a good job backing you up with supporting work? Have you made a number of sound decisions, which have only temporarily led you to this bottleneck? Have you strengthened a skill while involved in this troublesome situation? Just where, precisely, are your thinking, behaviors, and associations working for you?

Continue your non-striving, non-stop writing about these factors for the next few minutes. You're answering these questions, by the way, so you can examine the situation from a different perspective, not for positive thinking purposes.

Okay, you've put your situation down on paper, and have briefly examined the parts that are working. Your next bout of writing centers around the area where your thoughts and actions may be hurting you. If you need to quickly scan your previous writing for a minute or so, go ahead. But don't get caught in daydreaming or rewriting. Start, instead, to talk with yourself about the areas where you've contributed to this troublesome situation.

Perhaps your actions are based on assumptions that just aren't true. Maybe you've failed to carry through on a promise you made to yourself or to others. You've probably covered some of this material during the initial step of this exercise. If so, that's fine. Just quickly note it again and continue to comb through the situation for four or five minutes looking for other areas where you may have dropped the ball.

At this point, your pages look like a fillet, blackened with both the logical and emotional factors that make up the situation. While writing out your thoughts you may have even started to steer yourself toward some potential solutions. *Sometimes getting all these notions and facts out of your head and down on paper is enough to trigger new, constructive associations which may have been blurred as they remained in your head.*

If that's not the case, continue on and ask yourself one more question, "What other situations have I seen that *remind* me of this one?" In reminding yourself on the page, think about similarities from the situations in your own past, in the past of others, as well as similarities from fictional stories you've encountered ("My situation reminds me that scene from *Die Hard* where Bruce Willis drops the computer down the elevator shaft...").

Such wide-ranging remembering may seem nutty, but many top cognitive scientists believe it the key to creative thought. You might also think about metaphorical images from nature or science or the art world, if that'll help ("I continually take the same course of action, kind of like birds returning to their nesting area over and over. Why do they do that, and, what might I learn from them that I can use?")

Keep in mind, you're not looking for the perfect answer here. Instead, you're continuing to spray the page with possible ideas. If your situation triggers five different remembrances, jot them all down, even if they contradict each other.

For instance, suppose you're a new consultant and you're having a problem finding work. Naturally, you have little (or no) consulting work to draw upon, but you've gotten jobs in other ways. Write quickly about those ways which seem most like your present situation.

If your best remembrances come from nonwork situations ("This reminds me of the time I put together the yearbook in high school"), by all means scribble those situations onto the page. Don't be afraid of following the goofy, tangential stuff; it may lead some-where important.

For the rest of the time remaining, come to some kind of conclu-sion, even if you must force it. *Based on all the writing and thinking you've done in the past twenty minutes, what needs to be done next?*

Perhaps you've seen a problem blockage more clearly now, and you see you don't have the technical skills necessary to unclog it. You do, however, know a co-worker with the skills to handle it. What's the best way to approach this person? When will you ask her? How will you know when the job's done effectively? If things don't go as planned, what can you do next?

Remember, you're looking for a next step, a possible solution, something to try. Of course, a few more nights of writing, done for yourself alone, may generate the kind of fresh perspectives you'll need to come up with a good solution. Usually, though, *it's best to take some kind of real world action, no matter how slight, and weave the results into the next night's writing.*

This kind of writing is like the scientific method. You . . .

1. observe

2. hypothesize

3. experiment

4. note the results, and,

5. ask "What's next?"

Work until your alarm rings (Short of a medical emergency, never quit your private writing early!).

Points to Remember

- Vary the session-lengths and specific techniques used during your bouts of private writing.

- Talk to yourself, on paper, about any resistance you're feeling about your problem, or the private writing method itself ("I don't feel like doing this").

- Dumping a lot of details and information on the page often suggests a solution in and of itself.

- Let one period's writing suggest how to begin the next period's writing.

- End your writing session by telling yourself about the next real-world action you're going to take based on your writing (even if that action is "Do more writing on the subject tomorrow").

Try This: Write for twenty minutes about (1) How you're helping yourself at your job, and (2) How you're hurting yourself at your job. During the writing, remind yourself of ideas and situations that seem analogous to your present situation.

14

Embrace Novelty

Let's say you're ambitious. Let's say you've done your twenty minutes or so of private writing, but you—creative demon that you are—don't want to stop there. You enjoy this crazy business of hunkering down with your own thoughts. This private writing process, you discover, is exhilarating. You start with road-weary thoughts and write yourself into shiny new ones. While you're writing you find yourself, at times, laughing, because you're surprising yourself with flashes of brilliance. You want more, but you also want something different.

I applaud your hunger for novelty. The more ways you have of "playing" with your problem, the better. Why? Because we all have our favorite methods of problem solving that, at one time, worked, only now they don't. Or we take our favorite method and misapply it (Maslow: "To a man with a hammer, everything is a nail").

Okay, then, what should you do next? Here's a few things you might try:

Read through your work, *circling the words or phrases that "feel" right to you.* Get it? As you scan your work, certain parts will seem more interesting or practical than others. Those parts are what you mark.

Write comments to yourself in the margins, too, or on scratch paper.

If you've ended a train of thought early, and you want to go back and develop it, note that. If, upon a second reading, you see you were terribly wrong about something you felt terribly right about, note that, too.

Scan your circled words, your marginalia. Do these thoughts, taken from your own mind and experience, suggest any clues in how to deal with your troublesome situation?

Start your timer again for ten minutes or so, and speedily answer this question: "From all I've gathered, *what have I missed?*"

Is there a fact that you only now recall, but which seems pertinent? Have you said all you need to say at this point? Capture these straggler thoughts and dump them onto the page. Take a minute or two here and see what's missing.

You're now going to change perspective yet again, by examining the *worst and best case scenarios* inherent to your troublesome situation. First, the worst.

Ask yourself, "If things continue to go as they have, what's the worst that could happen to me?" Investigate this downward slide in incremental steps.

For instance, if you're late handing in a report, you may write something like:

> *My boss will scream at me, because my late report will hold up the entire presentation. Of course, the other people presenting with me will be pissed. They'll probably not speak to me for a few weeks. But if we lose the account, this might be just what the boss was looking for to let me go. I'll be fired. At my salary, it may be hard to find something at the same level and pay. I might be out of work for a while....*

Usually, we engage in this catastrophizing all the time, only we keep it murkily trapped in our minds, where it hangs out somewhere within the category of "being realistic."

On paper, though, our worst case scenario often looks like the foolish overexaggeration that it normally is. And if some of these worst case points continue to ring true to you, at least they're out on the table where you can plan for them ("If I might get fired, it's best to get my references lined up now while I still look pretty good").

Then it's on to a question equally fantasy-based, "What's the best that could happen to me?" Again, gradual steps up the insanely great ladder may give you some ideas you never before considered. If you're planning where to market a new widget, for instance, you might recall your success marketing an old widget, and build from there:

> *The thing that made the old widget fly was its "No down-time" guarantee. So if I repushed that point, and sold the new widget to the same old-widget-buying customers, that's a 1.8 million dollar profit right there. That's cool, but this new widget has a larger audience than just those previous customers. There's the automotive industry: four million bucks profit there. And don't forget the military. True, their budget's been cut, but that just means they need to be more productive with the budget they have. That's seven million bucks. And if I could sell it to our military overseas, perhaps I could somehow link up with our allies and pitch it to them....*

Answering this question requires playfulness, thoughtfulness, and the ability to follow ideas to their logical conclusion. If you don't laugh during this step, you haven't done it properly. Take a few minutes here, and see if you can't shake loose some solutions which had been trapped in your brain under the heading "naive" or "blue sky."

Of course, always end your session by reminding yourself about what you just learned, and give yourself an action step (no matter how small) to carry out in the world.

Before this chapter closes, I have two final points I'd like to make.

First: I've given you another potential framework within which to investigate your problem. Don't think, "These are *the* steps of private writing." No, no, no, no, no. This chapter, and the previous one, were examples of what you *might* do. I personally never do the steps in exactly the order I just laid them out for you in.

Which leads me to...

Second: *Whenever you feel something important happening in your writing, drop the timetable and structure and follow that thought.* Keep a strong sense of freedom during your search. If parts of the process seem confining, drop them. Bottom line: You're using the writing, here, as a way of creatively revisiting a blocked situation. Whatever helps you towards that end, use it.

Points to Remember

- Once your timer stops, go back through your writing and do two things: (1) circle intriguing words and concepts for future explorations, and (2) write margin notes to yourself about stated—and unstated—key points.

- Include best and worst case scenarios in your private writing, as well as an extensive look at ideas you missed on the first go-around.

  Try This: Go back through your last three private writings, and circle the concepts that seem to "speak" to you. Take the concept from this group that seems most powerful to you, and do thirty minutes' private writing on it.

15

Give Yourself Proof

When you first opened this book, at which point in the text did you begin to read? Did you start at page one, word one, and work your way through it until you reached this spot? Or did you, perhaps, peruse the Table of Contents, pick out one of the many curious chapter titles, and dive in there?

If I hadn't written this text, and instead came innocently upon it, here's the odd way I would have approached *Accidental Genius*: I'd have wrenched the book open somewhere in the middle and studied whatever page my eye fell to.

If I liked what I saw, I might have continued flipping forward, but I might just as likely have started riffling the text backward, and continued in a disturbingly non-linear, forward-reverse-forward-reverse manner, scanning a (somewhat) conceptually advanced passage on page 92, before I reached a simpler, building-block passage on page 5, which would then compel me to leap ahead to page 133 to see whether the author had developed his ideas sufficiently.

By my peculiar scanning method, I'd know a heck of a lot about *Accidental Genius*'s material, but I'd also be confused about its progression, even its fundamental philosophy.

Why, then, do I do that? What's the rationale behind my jumping?

Well, when I initially thought about it, I figured it stemmed from my desire to draw my own conclusions about a book's material. I assumed that if I dipped into the author's argument piecemeal, I wouldn't be lulled into agreeing with premises that weren't fully sound, and following those premises to faulty conclusions.

But that seemed too pat to be true, so I did some more noodling. I realized that I scanned like that because of my years spent paging through magic books.

See, the typical structure of a written magic trick explanation is "Effect," then "Method." That is, the magician-writer first explains what the trick looks like to the audience (the "Effect"), then he describes the secret means which accomplish the trick (the "Method"). Sometimes, in my insane desire to learn a fresh, empowering secret, I'd brush past the merely entertaining "Effect" part of the description, and head straight into the meaty "Method" section, in the arrogant hope of acquiring privileged secrets which could elevate me in the eyes of others.

Then I thought, Hey, maybe magic has nothing to do with it. Maybe I hopscotch like that because of my interest in baseball.

In fact, I can remember, at eight years old, paging through a much-loved souvenir book from the Baseball Hall of Fame, which contained photos of the players' bronzed ceremonial plaques alongside their abbreviated biographies. The very topography of the book, with its comb binding that allowed it to sit forever open at any page, giving the Hall's lesser members (say, Rabbit Maranville) the same democratic weight as its leading men (say, Babe Ruth), encouraged me to explore it in my own unique way—a way which I apparently imported when studying other books.

Enough.

Obviously, I couldn't possibly know, with supreme certainty, why I scan books in such an odd way. But, at least, I know that I don't know; In other words, I understand that most of my theories on this subject are based on speculation, association, faded memory, and jumbled reasoning.

Lots of people think they know a lot more about themselves than they really do. They have "knowledge" about themselves based on conclusions which they've creatively drawn—not from what's actually happened to them in their lives—but from cleverly constructed scenarios they've erected in their minds.

What's my point, then? It's this: while engaging in private writing, you will, at times, think you're uncovering the root cause of important problems, and triggering epiphanies about the way you, and others, act. If you do, fine. *Just keep doubt and skepticism open in your mind as to the brilliance of your revelation.* What today appears to be The Right Answer might tomorrow prove to be a false positive.

When you discover some key revelation, *ask yourself for tangible proof as to why you believe what you believe.* If your "proof" lies in the murky waters of, say, intuition, you'd better think twice about basing an important action on it.

If you do decide to use your revelation or epiphany as the basis for action, then, by all means, *follow the results of your actions through more private writing.*

The private writing page has a wonderful way of objectifying information, and keeps us honest about our competencies and inefficiencies—if we let it. In your writing ask yourself regularly why you believe what you believe, and demand proof. Don't take your own word at face value.

Points to Remember

- The mind is a trickster. Just because your written rationale *sounds* true, doesn't mean it is true. Give yourself proof.

- Test your head-spun insights in the real world, and follow the results through repeated rounds of private writing.

   Try This: Using the secrets of private writing, tell yourself about three instances where you were *certain* you were right, only to discover you were wrong.

16

The Benefit
in Growing Tired
of Yourself

I suffer from what a consultant friend calls "ideaphoria." That is, interesting ideas intoxicate me. In fact, I get so worked up over a good idea that my body often betrays my mind's hidden excitement; were you, for instance, to peek into my study, it wouldn't be odd for you to find me rocking in my chair, slapping my leg, and mumbling feverishly to myself —all while I was guzzling a particularly heady thought.

Until now, I've allowed my public ideaphoria to gallop relatively unbridled through these pages, as I've described for you the wonders of private writing. I've told you that, yes indeed, if you regularly engage in this practice, great things may happen for you in terms of job mastery and personal satisfaction. But in my honest rush to convince you of private writing's benefits, I may have given you the notion that such writing is one long, exhilarating slam-dance of radiant ideas. If I've given you that impression, I apologize.

Here, then, is the portly truth of the matter: While your private writing may contain your thinking at its best, it'll also contain it at its worst. And not only is your bad thinking on display in these writings, but your ineffectual behavior will also make many treacherous appearances, causing you to sink your head in your trembling hands.

Your private writings, in short, will remind you time and again that you're not always as predictably smart and productive as you believe yourself to be (Aren't you glad you bought this book?). You'll actually find yourself growing physically and mentally tired of your own thoughts and actions.

But wait: I have life-affirming news for you! These same writings that you thought would be your ruin, paradoxically, hold within them your salvation. *By studying those written points where your thoughts grow dry and your writing wilted, you may hit upon important indicators of what, and how, you need to change.*

This curious change-through-disgust-and-monotony phenomenon was first put into words for me during an interview I conducted with British poet and corporate speaker, David Whyte.

I know David Whyte is a poet because he can make you reevaluate your entire life while he recites a single stanza. That quality, good as it is, wouldn't put most poets in demand on the corporate speaking circuit, but Whyte is different. His telephone rings all year long with offers from multi-nationals who hire him to use poetry to effect change within their employees and in their markets.

When Whyte takes the podium at these corporate sessions, he tries to accomplish two things: (1) to get people interested in poetry, and (2) to get them to use poems as a way to engage in meaningful, business-centric conversation.

Let's say Whyte is called into Corporation X. He and X's managers come together and discuss a vital problem, including why the current back-and-forth isn't helping to solve things.

Based on what he hears, Whyte recites lines of poetry—from the works of Dante, Coleridge, William Carlos Williams, or any one of the hundreds of other poets whose work he's committed to memory—and leads a spirited discussion about the stalled problem, as seen through the metaphorical language of the poem. So an employee discipline problem gets run through the bracing imagery of, say, *Beowulf*, while an untapped marketing opportunity gets dunked into the briny symbolism of *The Rime of the Ancient Mariner.*

Suddenly, the people at Corporation X are discussing the problem in a way they never thought possible, and coming, one hopes, to an understanding that will translate itself into a workable business practice. Of the reactions his intervention gets, Whyte says, "People get excited when they have language for qualities and phenomena they didn't previously have. These people now have language for going into difficult places."

Whyte, in a sense, channels the wisdom of dead poets as a way to create an atmosphere of possibility in the bottom-line world of the twenty-first century corporate worker. Whyte understands that even complex global problems can be solved when people start speaking in ways just slightly differently than they're used to speaking.

So why am I telling you this?

Just as Whyte has firsthand experience that novel language and images force workers into fresh perspectives, he's also seen that *stereotyped change-motivations aren't always the most effective ways to generate change.* He revealed this to me, in an aside, while I was interviewing him about writing poetry:

> **Me:** "You have a love of many poets, of people like Coleridge, yet you want to write like yourself. How do you stop all these loves from interfering with your unique writing voice?"
>
> **Whyte:** "You start with imitation because you don't know how to do this [produce a poem]. These poets are doing astonishing things. So you find the ones you love—there's absolutely nothing wrong with writing pieces that are pure Ted Hughes or Seamus Heaney or Rilke—and you just keep writing your way into your own voice. Eventually, you realize that you're not writing Rilke or Heaney anymore, that there's another voice there which you, in Mary Oliver's words, 'slowly recognize as your own.'
>
> "That's actually a well recognized way of discovering your own voice—of imitating others until you get tired of imitating others.

"A lot of the poetic discipline boils down to getting tired of yourself, and I really believe that. When you get tired of yourself, then you change.

"See, *even if you're stuck in life, if you can describe just exactly the way you're stuck, then you will immediately recognize that you can't go on that way anymore. So just saying precisely, writing precisely, how you're stuck, or how you're alienated, opens up a door of freedom for you.*"

Whyte's language choices sent gong-like reverberations through my head. "Tired," "stuck," "alienated"—not the usual motivational words business people use when doping out their slick methodologies for change, but Whyte used them. These words seemed so unheroic, so petty, so selfish—but so true!

So the question becomes, how can we identify—and deal with productively—those tired elements in our own work lives?

Based on my own private writings, and on those of students who have shared their work with me, here are few hiding places for tiredness which you might like to investigate in your own jotting:

- You keep hearkening back to the same thoughts ("I really should finish X")

- ... the same people ("Janet is the key to finding a way out of this")

- ... the same images or metaphors ("The market is like a deodorant stick")

- ... the same language (you riddle a page with the phrase "buckle down" forty-two times)

- You race past ordinary-yet-distasteful scenes as quickly as you can ("I completed all my rancid paperwork today")

- You're continually self-critical ("I obviously stink"), or

- ... other-critical ("Barney obviously stinks")

- You believe you've tried out all possible solutions, and they've all left you wanting ("That's the tenth, and final, way that I know won't work")

- You assume that nothing can be done about a specific situation ("It's hopeless")

- While reading your work aloud (to yourself), your voice inexplicably hesitates, or wavers, at passage x.

Now, please don't eyeball a page or two of your private writing, notice one of these symptoms, and exclaim, "Zounds! I knew it! I am tired!" Or worse yet, start a fresh page of writing in which you "unintentionally" shoehorn in one, or more, of these symptoms and stun yourself with revelation.

Growing tired of yourself isn't a technique to practice, like calling a new prospect by his first name throughout the sales call. Instead, its value is in knowing that it exists—and it may be hiding out in the open, because you've been ignoring its song.

If you find tiredness' droppings, note how they've been deposited into your life. If those droppings don't make themselves plain on the page, don't crawl on your hands and knees trying to sniff them out.

So what is to be done if you find one of these above-listed symptoms, or, perhaps, one I've neglected to mention? At first, nothing. Becoming tired, bored, and disgusted with your situation is part of your nature, hardwired into you by divinity, evolution, or both. *At times, the best way to deal with being tired is to let yourself be tired.*

How, though, do you tell if your writing reveals points of destructive tiredness, or constructive plateauing? Back to David Whyte for the answer.

If you recall, he said:

> "See, even if you're stuck in life, if you can describe just
> exactly the way you're stuck, then you will immediately
> recognize that you can't go on that way anymore. So just say-
> ing precisely, writing precisely, how you're stuck, or how
> you're alienated, opens up a door of freedom for you."

Tattoo that word "exactly" into your mind—it's the private writer's best friend. If you put into words *exactly* how the project failed, *exactly* how the negotiations faltered, *exactly* how your career stumbled, magic happens. A lucidity creeps into your thinking; this lucidity may only come with several trips to the well of exact writing, but, believe me, it clears your head like a window thrown open.

Your head-clearing lucidity may point you in a number of directions. Maybe it will tell you that, yes, you're tired of situation X, things need to change, and here's a proto-plan. Or, based on what's come before, you're stepping across a mucky plateau, and the only thing that's needed is to push gamely ahead.

How, though, do you cast this spell known as "exact writing"?

Points to Remember

- If you put honest thinking into your written words, you spot situations that yawn to be changed.

  Try This: Write for ten minutes about a situation that physically and mentally exhausts you. Don't try to solve anything in this bout of writing, just get the details down.

17

The Magic of Exact Writing

I could ask you, right now, to put into words exactly how you're tired, or precisely how you're stuck. And if I asked you to do that, you know what you'd put on the page? Fairy tales.

To ask you to talk about your situation—with exacting, surgical precision—is just about as impossible as drawing a foot-wide circle on the ground, and asking a skydiver to hit it.

First, you can never know your own motivations for certain, much less know the motivations of others.

Second, growing tired happens over time; to ask you to make a summarizing statement about a fairly long-standing, meandering problem would be ludicrous.

Third, to ask you to boil down your situation would rob you of the very way out of it: churning it over in your mind, from different angles, so that myriad previously unseen perspectives suddenly lie exposed to the light.

The way, then, to write "exactly" about being tired isn't the impossible work of parsing your thoughts into one cutting laser-beam of accuracy. Instead, it's about dumping eighteen pounds of words onto paper, and making sure you're living those words as you write them.

Here's the same answer, rendered clearer through anecdote. Back in the mid-1960s, before even a sentence from *The Right Stuff* or *Bonfire of the Vanities* ever flashed inside his mind, Tom Wolfe was struggling for a way to approach a particularly unconventional magazine article he longed to write.

Wolfe wanted to profile a hot rod and custom car designer who soberly, and artistically, approached his freak-show craft. Wolfe knew this was an important human interest and societal critique story, but he didn't know how to coax it into words.

With the magazine's deadline about to steamroll him, Wolfe called his editor and came clean about his tired, hopeless state. About that conversation, Wolfe writes:

> "O.K., he [the magazine's editor] tells me, just type out my notes and send them over and he will get somebody else to write it. So about 8 o'clock that night I started typing the notes out in the form of a memorandum that began, 'Dear Byron' [his editor's name]. I started typing away, starting right with the first time I saw any custom cars in California. I just started recording it all, and inside of a couple of hours, typing like a madman, I could tell something was happening... The details themselves, when I wrote them down, suddenly made me see what was happening." [*The Kandy-Kolored Tangerine-Flake Streamline Baby*, p. xii]

After a marathon eight-and-a-half hour, uncensored writing session, a sleepless Wolfe took his "notes" over to the magazine, where they promptly scratched the "Dear Byron" salutation, and published the entire 49 pages (rather than the two-page article it was supposed to be). Thus began the distinctive style of one of the world's finest writers.

To us, of course, the publishing-success part of the story is unimportant. What we do need to pay attention to is Wolfe's manic, non-stop writing style, and the principles he used to make to make that style fly. Of particular note, let's examine Wolfe's

…*audience* for the memorandum,

…his use of the phrase "*recording it all,*"

…and his attention to *detail*.

The audience. By "audience," I mean the person who Wolfe addressed the memorandum to: Byron Dobell, the managing editor at *Esquire* magazine. Now, should you address your own writings to Mr. Dobell, or other prominent editors, in the hope that your style will set a brush fire through the literary world, and burn all the way up the bestseller lists? (It's okay if you answered yes, although, for the sake of the lesson, let's assume you answered no.)

For the most part, other than yourself, you'll have no audience for your writing—and that's the way it should be. Your private writing is confidential, for your eyes only, and you should strike out with fists and feet at anyone who feels the need the sneak a peek at your thoughts.

But what if you tried directing your thoughts toward someone else, even if this "someone else" never saw your writing? Do you think such a mind game would affect the direction of your ideas? You'd better believe it would.

Try this: Fix a subject in your mind, a subject about which you consider yourself an expert. Now, if I asked you to give a 250-second speech about it to a roomful of surgeons, how might you tailor the information to make it interesting to them? Even if the material doesn't lend itself to overt customization (*How would I apply my origami expertise to cardiologists, without seeming like an ass?*), the fact that you'll be speaking to a highly educated group certainly alters the way you'd talk (I can use words like 'laity' and 'recalcitrant').

Now give your speech to a roomful of high school students. Certainly, high school students can be as smart as the proverbial whip, but you couldn't possibly deliver your high-level, surgeon-specific speech to a roomful of youngsters who doodle on their sneakers and fling things that came out of their noses, could you? You'd have to recast what you say (*I can fold this paper into the shape of Cameron Diaz*), and dumb down your language (*I can tell them that the paper is blue*). And by altering what you do and say, you'd be thinking about your material in a different way, based upon the characteristics of the audience.

Consider, then, this idea of varying audience in your own writing —particularly as you try to write precisely about a tired situation (almost like "holding a paper conversation," only your audience remains silent but attentive).

Wolfe certainly saw his material through new eyes, as the magnetic force of "Dear Byron" exerted its steady pull on his thought selection. The act of private writing may start crunching some fresh creases into your brain, if that writing is directed in a never-to-be-sent, "talking letter" to your boss, spouse, friend, enemy, controller, salesperson, marketer, warehouse employee, janitor, favorite actor, hated actor, or a figure in history. If you give an honest effort to altering your audience as an experiment, you can't help but write yourself into some unexplored perspectives.

Recording it all. Because Wolfe was uncertain about how to shape his material, and because he didn't know what was critical and what was marginal, he spewed everything he could recall about the story down onto paper (49 sheets' worth, remember?). To use his own words, he "recorded it all."

Now what did Wolfe mean by invoking the word "recorded"? When I think of that word, I get a picture of an accountant dutifully entering a number in a large, brown leather ledger; no judgments or pondering, just hand movement. And that's exactly what I think Wolfe did, and what I'd like you to do.

While you're examining your tired situation, "record," or put onto the page, everything that pops up into your mind—whether it seems germane to the problem or not. If you want to judge what you're recording, by all means, do it, but do it without crossing out what you've written, criticizing yourself without questioning why you deserve that criticism, or stopping to phrase your thoughts more appropriately.

Think of "recording it all" as a heuristic that encourages you to articulate the unarticulated. In the same way that it's not up to the accountant to alter the number she's entering because she doesn't approve of that number, it's also not up to you to alter your thoughts as they appear: Disapprove of them, if you like, in the sentence that burps from your pen tip, but don't banish them to the vapors of the unsaid.

Details. So far I've told you that, according to David Whyte, describing "exactly" about a situation that's mentally exhausted you will help you change the situation—either through your attention to its workings, acceptance of its existence, or via the overt change strategies you create to bust it up.

I've also told you that, by examining Tom Wolfe's approach to a similar problem, the way to write "precisely" about your situation is not through the careful, edited language, but by choosing fresh audiences to help draw fresh perspectives from you, and by recording all thoughts as they burst into your consciousness. Now I will tell you this: *The most telling thing you'll find in the Wolfe excerpt is the sentence, "The details themselves, when I wrote them down, suddenly made me see what was happening."*

Details get a bad rap. When we say, "Attend to the details," it's said almost as a rebuke, as a caution to keep our minds on our work and not foul things up as we've done in the past. But, God is in the details. That is, looking at things closely reveals a—hold on for this—paradoxical simplicity and complexity that makes most anything fascinating, if not beautiful.

That last statement, abstract enough to float off the page like a lost balloon, needs to be brought back to earth. Let me make that point this way:

Say you serve as a marketer for a publisher, and one of your jobs is to e-mail your accounts about upcoming media appearances for your company's books.

That sounds important, but most of the information you normally send is bland stuff, a brief title mention in a regional newspaper, or an author's late night radio appearance. Consequently, you drag your Internet-driven heels, turning to other projects, rather than attend to the detail it takes to put together a credible e-mail. Your inaction eventually breeds more inaction, until you find yourself incapable of clicking your mouse.

During a spirited session of private writing, you address this tired issue, calling it "a barbell that cuts into my shoulders, and weighs me down all the day long." As a kind of experiment, though, you decide that since your company's books aren't getting more interesting, and your authors aren't becoming more newsworthy, you'll research ways to spice up your e-mails, and create some kind of value for you and your customers.

You hit the bookstore and the library, scoring a handful of texts on how to add zing to your electronic communiqués. Pen at the ready, you underline information on how to grab reader interest and sustain it throughout the letter. After blowing through a stack of scrap paper, you put together a letter that's better "than my standard dead fish." You send it, and do some followup. Not everyone has read your letter, but some people have. You talk to these people, and find out about the kinds of information they need to make a success of your company's books.

One of the store owners clues you in on several Usenet groups centered around the subjects which your company's books are noted for: Perhaps you could investigate some direct marketing to these groups. You're off to buy new books, make calls, perform experiments.

Through your private writing and your real-life experience, you're discovering that you'd stopped paying attention to your tired situation in any meaningful way; you had, in your mind, filed it under "bore," and there it stayed. By getting into the details of what bored you and how you might possibly use that boredom as a starting point for a new direction, you've made that situation come alive again, only this time you're making it work for you.

Have I made it clear, then, that writing in detail—about anything—elevates the subject out of the abstract class (i.e., automobile), and into a hard nuts-and-bolts reality where our minds can rap their mental knuckles against it (i.e., a red Firebird, with black leather seats, and a small American flag on the antenna snapping in the wind)?

Before you power-up your laptop and do a private writing about this chapter, here's a brief checklist of suggestions that you may want to play around with in your bouts of "exact" writing:

- Start your writing at the spot in the problem that most befuddles you. Ask yourself, why is there blockage here?

- Record your current thoughts about the situation, as well as your thoughts when the situation first arose. How do they differ, and why?

- Mentally peruse the situation and see if you've included everyone who belongs in it.

- When you're trying to analyze the behavior of others, stick to writing about their observable behavior; although we often believe we know what others are thinking, we, in fact, don't.

- If you're having trouble reliving the situation on paper, follow the wise advice of Peter Elbow, who tells his students: "To hell with words, see something" [*Writing with Power,* p. 336]

What Elbow means is, put yourself into the experience as vividly as you can. What counts is that you *see, hear, touch, smell,* and *taste* the situations you're visiting, and that you render those strong experiences in the most vivid, concrete language you have. Perhaps now, given your private writing-induced perspectives on things, you'll come to a possible answer that eluded you initially.

- Don't assume your tired situation is something to be "solved." It may be necessary to play it out as it stands. Or, it may fix itself.

97

- Question yourself as to whether you've really tried a certain solution, or if you just think you know how it'll turn out. Often, we think we've tried things which our minds have prematurely discounted.

Points to Remember

- Exact writing—that is, getting to the very heart of an important matter—requires you to flood the paper with words that honestly, and graphically, depict what you're thinking, seeing, and feeling about the matter. Exhaust yourself during the writing, in the hope that a few of your words ring true and suggest a solution.

- Use a variety of people as a focusing force in your writing.

- The most reliable way to be honest in your writing is to use lots of physical detail and kitcheny description of what you're thinking. If your mind tells you to write X, write X, even if writing Y would have made more logical sense.

Try This: Do ten minutes' writing about a crappy situation, but before you begin, address the page to someone involved in the difficulty (i.e., "Dear Sharon"). Write to the person in exacting detail—dumping as much info on the page as you can. When the timer rings, do another ten minutes' writing about the crappy situation, only this time address your remarks to someone who's involved in one of your cool situations. See if focusing on this person helps you re-see the tough situation.

18

Extract Gold from a Business Book

In this chapter you'll be learning how to study a business book and make its potentially valuable concepts your own—by agreeing and arguing with them on your private writing paper. If the book's ideas are strong, you'll have a greater sense of ownership over them, even knowing how to test them out in your own life. If the book's ideas stink, then you'll gain by refuting those ideas. You must actively engage with the material, and make it move. That's a key to this chapter, this book, this approach.

Okay, you need a book. I say this, not in the flippant manner of my Little League teammates, who, when I made an errant throw to first base intoned, "Good one, Levy!" Instead, I mean, with all seriousness and respect, you need a business book with a premise that intrigues you, one you'll want to give a close reading. No sense in torturing yourself with a work repellent to you.

As you work your way through the book, doctor its innards with your underlining and private notations. *Don't respect the book as a physical object. Customize it.* When you come to a sentence that stops you, a paragraph that makes you think, a fact that you may want to consult, highlight it in some way so you can put your finger on it again.

What you're doing here is corralling material that resonates to you, that sets your "Spider Sense" tingling. You're ticking off pieces of the book which strike you as out of the ordinary. Also, your ever-circling pen is keeping you alert, forcing you to pay attention to the author's ideas, even if his prose style may not justify it.

If, while reading, you have questions you'd like to ask the author, write them out in the book's margin. The same thing with an insight. Don't wait to put your thought into words, assuming that it's so $E=mc^2$-brilliant that you'll retain it in your mind forever. You won't (if someone kicks your chair leg, the brilliant thought will pop irretrievably out your ear hole). Rather, scribble it onto the page, even if you have to obscure the original text in doing so.

Don't, by the way, be stingy with your underlining, because if you don't save the book's vibrant material now, it'll be dead to you once you shut the cover. I'm being realistic. There's too much to read, learn, and do in this life, and unless a volume stands out as particularly worthy, you'll probably only thumb through it again to consult your highlights. The rest of the text might as well not be there.

At some point during this customizing process, you'll have a book containing thousands of words that mean nothing to you, and a few words which warrant some follow-up cogitating. Perhaps you'll want to read through the entire book before engaging in private writing. More than likely, though, your opinion-generating glands will start secreting as you come upon an interesting topic, and force you to forsake the reading temporarily. By all means, give in to your secretion: strip the intriguing piece of prose from the text, or encapsulate it in your own words, slap it onto your computer screen, and bang out ten to twenty minutes of non-stop opinion and excitement.

Let me give you an example of what I'm talking about. I've opened my own electronic private writing file on William J. Hudson's *Intellectual Capital*, and I'm paging through ten screens, expressing my intrigue, delight, and occasional consternation with Hudson's views. Here's one passage that "spoke to me," and my answer back to it:

"...it is a false hope that the world can be simplified into a handful of discrete propositions called trends or megatrends. The world is simply not obligated to do this. It need not kneel to human intelligence. And to believe that you can come to possess 'master ideas' may blind you to what you can do, which is barely outdistance your competitors (in the nick of time)." (Hudson, p. 212)

What is Hudson saying here? I think it's this: The world is ridiculously (yet appropriately) knotted—full of processes that function in tension against each other. For us to think we can sum up such a complex system in a few words (the very basis of a megatrend) is a grand display of hubris, and must be inaccurate.

These processes don't slow down or simplify so we can study and classify them. They proceed in the way that they proceed. Some things in this life just aren't comprehensible; that doesn't mean we should give up attempts to grasp our world, or swallow back all pronouncements and grand projections; it's just that we should be aware that our pronouncements are almost certainly screening us from most of the picture.

In this Hudson excerpt, he finishes by saying "what we can do" is "barely outdistance" competitors. What he means here, if I'm reading this correctly, is that once we realize that megatrends do as much to blind us as to what's happening, we can still use the knowledge and judgment we have to get done what we need to, just before our competitors beat us to it.

Could Hudson be wrong here? It's hard for me to argue against him.

I've always felt that people who make long term predictions were basically writing fiction in public, but doing it under the guise of telling the truth.

The best way to argue against Hudson is to say this: if you declare a trend, even to yourself, and work to make it happen, it could happen—and in that way, it helps, as a generating tool. If I say that I see more people are going to the theater, and I build a theater to capitalize on this trend, and work my kishkas off getting people into that theater and make it successful, then I guess my pronouncement would be a kind of self-fulfilling prophecy. A creative delusion that works to help me. Something to strive toward.

How could I use this idea in my own life? Not every idea needs to have immediate, practical use. But if I put some effort into seeing it with pragmatic specs, then maybe I'll have an easier time remembering it when it might come in handy. My answer, then: I don't go around announcing trends, but maybe I sometimes act on the world as if certain trends, or shall I call them assumptions, are true.

I know, for instance, if a certain sales account of mine has a history of giving me a two hundred dollar order, I think of them as a two hundred dollar account, and treat them accordingly— small-time: I'm not as forthcoming with special information, I may not stay as late as I should to help them, etc. My actions, in effect, are guaranteeing the growth of this account stay stunted. If I combed my client list and noted where I'm working to keep revenues small, I could try experimenting by giving these accounts a two thousand dollar effort.

I get the feeling I'm trying to turn Hudson's words into a self- help concept here, rather than using them to deal with the world at large, which is what he intended. But let me just remind myself that trend-watchers and I both think we have the world's number, we know how it'll behave, and our assumptions and projections might just be flat-out wrong.

Another example? Here, then, is my attempt to bring some personal meaning to a paragraph culled from Philip Crosby's book, *The Absolutes of Leadership:*

"If quality is defined in more traditional words such as 'goodness' and 'delight,' no one knows what it means. Quality then becomes an 'I know it when I see it' kind of thing. People will argue about how good something has to be. It is much better to have people discuss requirements and deal with specifics rather than emotions." (Crosby, p. 78)

I know there's been a lot of debate about "quality," and about the validity of that practice (Wow, I sound formal. Certain subjects draw that voice out). Malcolm Balderidge Award– winning companies have even gone out of business, only years after having proved that they were mandarins of quality control. But Crosby has a solid point in stating people should deal in "specifics rather than emotions" (emotions, though, is an unfortunate word choice here; emotions often have a lot to do with the specifics of what's recognized as quality).

As long as people stay with flabby generalities ("I like this way of doing business because it's good"), there's nothing to discuss or work with. So too, If I say something ambiguous, like "Process X should be done faster," that's only a starting point for improving Process X.

Some meaningful questions accompanying "Process X should be done faster," would be provocations like, "Faster? How much faster? What would faster look like to you? Why does it need to go faster? Would going faster be something our customers would notice? Would going faster in Process X pull resources away from another part of our business and damage us there? What if we dropped Process X altogether? Would an improvement in Process X have a beneficial carry-over effect to any of our other processes? How would we make Process X faster? What are ten different ways we could make Process X better? Which of these ten answers holds the most promise, and why? If we applied one of these answers, how would we know if it was working? How would we decide to keep this new method

*as a regular part of Process X? If we had to excise our
'improvement' out of Process X, would we have to explain its
removal to our customers? If we did remove this 'improvement,'
how would we explain our decision to others? If this
improvement worked, how could we leverage it and use it in
other parts of our business?"*

I hear you, with eyes bulged in fear (or boredom), asking yourself, "Is Mark actually going to answer all these questions?" Of course not.

The point here is not to make unnecessary work for ourselves by manufacturing endless questions. The point is to know that all these questions can rightfully be asked, and most of them should be asked, even if they only generate a one- or two-sentence response. The rule to follow is this: During private writing, always wrestle with a subject where it holds the most energy for you.

If, in your own writing, you formulate a question that excites you, take off after it like a dog after a rabbit. You can always look back after your sprint, and fill in those yeoman parts of your quest that need filling in. That's part of the beauty of using writing to help you figure out problems: the writing doesn't withdraw itself after it flashes upon the page. Don't make your task grim. These private writing moments should be among the most invigorating of your day—like rubbing your mind down in a rough towel. Back to my private writing:

*All this talk of requirements and specifics is hunky-dory, but
a full-scale, consultant-driven quality intervention is not going
to happen where I work. I remember years back bringing in
Crosby's people for a look-see at our place, but the bosses didn't
think it warranted the expense. And maybe they were right.*

*How, though, can I suck the marrow out of these quality
bones? How can I apply the good information in this excerpt to
what I do?*

*Well, on a sales level, I can bug my customers about what
constitutes quality in their dealings with me. What specifics*

cause them to say, "Mark and his company are outstanding," and what specifics cause them to say, "I wish Mark and his company did this better."

Better write up a checklist of subjects to talk about with my clients, since people might forget to tell me about a specific that doesn't jump readily to mind. What would be on my checklist?

Sales: Do we speak often enough? Too often? Do I bring up the necessary books and information? What else could I be doing for them? What do other companies do for them? Are our terms good?

Shipping: Do our books get to their stores when they expect them to arrive? Is this quick enough? Are our boxes sturdy? Is the packing material doing its job? Are the invoices clear?

Marketing: Do they need materials from us? Are they aware of all the co-op policies out there, and are they taking advantage of them? Do they ever access our web page, and does it have anything on it they can use?

Accounting: Are we helpful and easy to deal with?

Obviously, I'll need to talk with the heads of other departments before conducting my little survey. I'm sure there are important questions I should be asking, but haven't thought of (Yes, returns!). I'll also make it a point to try to get my clients to give me stories about good and bad service they've received from us. Sometimes, a vivid story reveals more than a list of properties divorced from a flesh-and-blood situation."

Notice how I took a concept largely unusable from where I stood in my organization, and extracted as much as I could from it.

After debating with the Crosby excerpt, I had something of an understanding of what he was getting at (although Crosby himself may dispute that), and, more important, I had an plan of action based on the ideas I had dissected. Yes, I did go through with the plan you see written here; it did generate results; and I tracked those results on the home field of my private writing page.

Points to Remember

- Customize business books as you read them: underline; dog-ear; question; argue; agree vehemently; write in the margins and on the blank end papers. You're reading the book in order to get workable ideas, and the best way to ferret out the workable ideas is to be active as you read.

- Through writing, try applying the author's ideas to your own life. Even if you disagree with what the author says, that disagreement suggests that you know what should be done. Write about this knowing.

Try This: Pick the idea you find most, and least, valuable in this book, and write for ten minutes on each.

19

Write Your Way into Solutions (A Demo)

Remember a while back, when I explained that private writing isn't done with any set strategy in mind, but is improvised as you go along? I then followed up that advice with two process chapters (*Drop Your Mind on Paper* and *Embrace Novelty*) that gave you a picture of what a couple of writing sessions might look like. Well, I was secretly holding something back from you—only I was doing it with good reason.

The thing I was holding back? A student's private writing sample in which he explicitly follows the framework I laid out for you in those chapters. The question is, of course, why didn't I show you his writing then? Because I didn't want you to become locked into that provisional format.

I figured if I showed you this long private writing sample after those chapters, I'd be sending you the implicit message that "this is really the way to do it," despite my admonishment that those chapters only offered a sample structure. Now, though, I think you're ready.

Now I think you'll read this private writing sample and realize it's just a demonstration of one way to do it. Try your hand at everything in this book. You'll develop favorite approaches, naturally, but don't get locked into a stale routine.

The following sample was written by a bookstore manager who was procrastinating about looking for new work. He still enjoyed parts of his job, but, in general, he felt unchallenged.

If the writing here seems clear and flowing, don't be fooled: it's been edited so you can more easily understand each step. During the original effort (which took thirty minutes), the writer wrote portions of this in a short-hand form which only he would understand (using "kitchen language," sentence fragments, etc.).

Also, be aware that this was only the first in a long series of writings he did on this topic.

Students new to this process think they can solve their problems, and uncover opportunities, with one session's writing. I wish it were that simple. Because our lives are endlessly complex and changing, you'll find that this process works best on a regular basis. Maybe twice a week, or twice a day. But *as you begin to draw upon your own wisdom through these writings, you'll find yourself scheduling more time to engage in them.*

1. The situation dump

I'm investigating some ideas about changing my career. Actually, more to the point: I'm investigating, through this writing, why I'm sticking around in a job I find to be a crashing bore. I actually haven't looked around anywhere for a change yet, and I don't know if I'm a coward because of it, or prudent.

I've been doing a strong job at the store since I started here four years ago. But I've proved to my boss, and more importantly to myself, that I've done all I can do here. I mean, I think I've hit thirteen of sixteen quarters I've been here, and that ain't shabby. It's just, "Come on already." This place is one challenge I've shown I'm better than and can neatly put behind me. Why am I finding it so hard to get my motor cranking to look elsewhere?

2. What's working here?

I guess since I'm doing a bang-up job, I've got plenty "working." My boss respects my ability to upkeep high standards. She knows I can sell a book. Hell, she knows I'm impassioned about it. She also knows that while the store's had some personnel issues, I've handled them, if not perfectly, at least adequately. Also, she doesn't hang over me, like she does with some of the other managers. Besides going over the weekly dollar figures with her by phone, I rarely even see her. That's a good element—she trusts me.

I get to people watch. That's a bonus...The customers are pretty savvy and pleasant... My assistants are all top notch... My pay is okay... What else?...

Yes, I'm doing something I excel at. Let's not gloss over that. Just because I'm feeling stale, I shouldn't lose sight of the fact that I'm making my company nearly three million dollars a year, I'm helping to educate people, and the customers tell me they look forward to hanging out and buying from my store. I should try and remember that those things aren't givens; they don't happen automatically.

3. How am I hurting myself?

I'm hurting myself by not stretching. I'm doing a better job than average, yes, but I've got to keep myself from going to sleep on the job by downing four cups of coffee a day and playing little games with myself ("Let's see, how many carts of books can the staff shelve today?"). That's not a way to live. And I know that eventually I'll run out of those little escalating games to play, and then what?

I've somehow convinced myself that it's safe staying here, that there'll never be competition, that dollar totals will always go up.

But if I'm losing interest on doing a good job, something has got to give. And how can my inattention and inaction then be safe? What's the saying? If you stand still, you'll get run over.

4. What's the situation remind me of?

This reminds me…of…of when I tried to learn how to swim, as a kid. I wouldn't let go of dry land the whole time I was in the pool. Dad would try to teach me, and I think I wanted to learn. But I always stayed by the pool's walls, and grabbed onto the railing whenever things got a little trying for me. To this day I can't swim, because I never gave it a true shot.

And this job is like those failed swimming lessons. I'm holding onto something I know, and if I dabble in looking for something else, I'll probably never find anything. I've got to let go of the railing, my job. Of course, that doesn't mean I'll outright quit, but I think I need to go a bit more public in my efforts, and put in a bit more work in earnest. My cousin always said that the water will hold you up if you let it, and maybe the same thing is true in looking for new work. If I make an honest effort, maybe the natural buoyancy of the situation (like my good work ethic) will hold me up and see me through so I can excel in another job.

5. Circling key words and phrases

This student circled the following words and phrases on his paper:

"Coward"…"prudent"…"high standards"…"not perfectly"…"I'm doing something I excel at"…"these things aren't givens"…"four cups of coffee a day"…"little escalating games"…"my good work ethic will hold me up."

In light of these selections, he wrote the following note to himself:

Maybe I'm a perfectionist, even though I've never thought of myself in that way before. Lots of the words I circled kind of lean towards always being the best and always staying on top of

things. Those aren't realistic goals, and my coffee and head
games are proof of that.

6. What have I missed?

What have I missed? I don't think anything. Let me see. Let
me see. I'll try harder. I missed writing about moving up in my
company's hierarchy. I think I'm supposed to write about that at
the end of this exercise, but I'll think about it now.

If I laid my problem on the line for my boss, that might make
me look like a bit of a weakling (there's that perfectionism), or
she might sympathize with me and put me in for a transfer to
the front office. Would I like it there? Only if I got to work with
the books. No computer or number job for me. So I guess I see
just how important working with books is to me. I either need a
job where that's built into it, or I need to build it in. That's what
I missed.

7. Indulging the dark side (worst case scenarios)

Hello!, this part is easy. My brain has an enormous worst
case scenario capacity. So let's see... If I continued to work there,
I'd use my shoelaces to hang myself. If I continued to work at the
store, my work would continue to slip. I'd not only be fired, but
I'd also have a shameful, lousy reference to draw upon, if I could
draw upon it at all. I'd have to take some kind of journeyman job,
possibly away from books. Since I often let inertia take over, I'd
remain in this lousy journeyman job for years, perhaps for all
time. I couldn't, of course, keep my nice apartment on my
journeyman salary, so I'd have to move into a place where you
can hear the neighbors playing music and stomping on your
ceiling. Okay, and what could happen if I asked my present boss
to move me up to the home office? My boss could sit on my
request, and make my life miserable by using the information

against me, thus forcing me to quit, and starting the journeyman thing again.

Tomorrow, I'll definitely write about preventing any of these scenarios from happening. They may be stupid, but they really do illustrate how I think.

8. How good can it get? (best case scenarios)

I could make up a resume, start a remarkably insightful conversation with one of these publishing people who stop in the shop, and land a job as an editor or a marketing person. I could help develop young authors, and get involved in helping some of the writers whose work I've loved all these years.

I would sit in my office, manuscript pages piled high, and write notes in the margins about the characters' motivations and how to punch up the fifth chapter.

I'd go out to lunch with the authors, visit bookstores, sit on panels, and write articles for Harper's about the current state of fiction. I'd be very much respected and appreciated by the writers themselves, and by people in general, once they heard about the job I do.

9. Alternatives (asking yourself, what's next?)

So what's workable here? The negative stuff was much easier to write, since I think about that part of my life quite a bit, and let the positive and potentially positive go blurry. If I think about it, though, I can certainly see some small next steps I can take.

For one thing, I can scout out a career counselor and get some help from them. I guess that's a fairly obvious step, but I never thought about it before. I'll take a look in the "Careers" section of the store for potential counselors to approach. I know some of them specialize in supposedly objective measures, like aptitude and interest tests. Others are more like therapists, I think, and they somehow talk with you to find out what and where you'd do best. So that's step one.

I wrote about resumes. That seems a bit daunting to me, trying to sum all my work up in a tight group of sentences. What I can do is write down some of my accomplishments, figures and such. Then, maybe the career counselor can give me a few pointers on how to structure the stuff for maximum oomph.

I can also talk to the publishing people who currently come into the store. I know, off the top of my head, four people who I could strike up a pretty blatant conversation with. Of course, I need to think about what to ask them. I mean, if I say "I'm looking for a job," that's way too unfocused, and a bit desperate sounding. Maybe if I prefaced the conversation with a few credentials ("This store has run over plan 80% of the time I've managed here. I think I've done my job"), that might make me seem I have more to offer than begging for a job.

I don't think I'll approach my boss yet. After the counselor, maybe. If I did it now, and she turned me down, I'd be real unclear as to my options. It's much better for me to have a few alternate paths, investigate them, and then make my move.

So I'll check out those career books for the next week, and have a counselor in two. Done.

10. More decent notions

This student ended by circling these words:

"work with books"... "preventing journeyman"... "publishing people"... "current state of fiction"... "careers section"... "list accomplishments"... "credentials."

Points to Remember

- Besides the six secrets to fuel your private writing, there are no set-in-stone bylaws you should use each time you power up.

  Try This: Comb through this book, and make a list of all the secrets, techniques, and strategies you find. Now craft a couple of writing line-ups from what you found ("Let's see. I'll start with 'try easy,' segue into 'go with a thought,' follow up with 'holding a paper conversation,' and finish with 'what's next?'"). Use them for ten-, twenty-, thirty-, and forty-minute exercises based on your cool and crappy observations.

20

You Are What You Focus On

This chapter might not seem to be about writing, but it is.

While still in my teens, I came across a quote that has stuck with me. The words were Emerson's, and the philosopher had written, "Make the most of yourself, for that is all there is of you."

In my gangly enthusiasm, I neatly copied those words onto an index card, carefully folded the card into quarters, and carried it as a sort of literary smelling salts, to be inhaled when I needed a rush of pragmatic bravado for those situations in which I felt overmatched.

I wish I could tell you that the quote radically altered my life, that Emerson's spirit blew hot across the century, filling my lungs with his transcendental fury, but it didn't. I probably tossed the index card when it made my wallet too fat to sit on.

But here's how the spirit of the quote did stick, and help me work *gradually* towards the things I find important:

Emerson's words marked the first time I ever realized that if I was ever going to do anything that mattered with my life, I had to use whatever fixed mental and physical capacities I was born with. That is, unless I put in effort, I wasn't going to suddenly become smarter, more athletic, or a greater success.

Emerson's words also signified the first time I started valuing the contents of my mind—not because my intellect was a raging force of nature that leveled anything in its path, but because, again, that's what I had been given to work with.

I realized that if I wanted to write books, I had to be the type of person who focused on book-writing types of activities (reading, grammar, journalistic techniques, etc.). If I wanted to be a salesman, I had to focus on salesman-type activities (prospecting, getting favorable attention, establishing rapport, etc.). The skills I needed to do these things weren't going to drop on me while I slept, like benevolent airborne spores. I had to focus on them.

My focus, in a sense, has defined who I am. Because I've spent so much time throwing my attention to the publishing field, I haven't, for instance, become a landscape architect or a baseball player. Because I enjoy using my leisure time to study magic, I spend little time studying stamp collecting or knife throwing.

My particular focus has other crucial implications for my life. Not only does my attention dictate what subjects I spend my time and effort investigating, it also tells me how I should investigate them. Geoff Bellman, an astute management consultant, expressed this thought beautifully when he wrote:

> "Having spent my early years in a training department, I was disposed to think of performance problems as training problems. Especially in the realm of management behavior or interpersonal behavior, I 'knew' that if someone was not doing something very well, it was because he or she didn't know how and merely needed training. And of course, I was a trainer, so wasn't that nice for both of us? Not surprisingly, now that I don't do much training anymore, I see it differently." (*The Consultant's Calling*, p.129)

I, too, approach situations wielding my own focus-based biases. Rather than beginning with an unadorned view of a problem, I suspect that my mind starts me at a favorite, rut-worn set point, and sends me searching for solutions from there.

All my talk of focus, so far, sounds overtly ominous, with its life-changing paths taken and ignored. Focus, however, decrees what I see, or don't see, even in mundane ways.

Just the other day I realized there was a Post-It note stuck to the edge of my workplace computer screen. Now, this note didn't suddenly erupt, like a pimple on a shiny face. I stuck it there myself, ten months earlier.

I had this note in my line of sight 40+ hours a week, week after week, and I only focused on it when I inadvertently jostled my terminal. For whatever reasons, Post-It notes don't interest me, at least not those affixed to the rim of my computer screen.

I, in some ways, know how I operate, and I "know" that if that Post-It note had critical information on it, I would have stuck it in the center of the computer screen, or onto the keyboard keys. If something really needs to be done, I want it to get in my way, to hound me, to stay in the Big Top of my attending mind.

This poor curling Post-It, which had seen spring turn to winter, and winter turn to summer, and its penciled message—"Get videotapes and books back from David"—was potent enough that I didn't want to forget it, but mild enough that it never pushed me across the threshold of action. For approximately 200 working days, then, my focus looked past that Post-It and told me there were better things to attend to.

Do these focus-related thoughts of mine get a smile of recognition from you, or are you mentally tossing them to the floor and stubbing them out with your heel? Although I've yet to let you get a word in this chapter, my focus certainly hasn't left you. If you and I were sitting together in a room right now, I would ask you to relate your stories, big and small, regarding focus.

You might tell me what you do for a living, what your hobbies are, what your family life is like. We'd order in pizza. You'd continue by telling me what gets you fired-up mad, and switched-on happy. I'd ask what part you thought your private focus played in these matters, and whether altering your focus would alter the way you lived your life. I'd study your words, and your excitement, for proof that this concept had "taken" in your mind, that you believed it fully.

Whether I sensed that you believed it or not, I'd offer up one small exercise, a kind of magic trick, to give you the experience of attention-alteration while we were sitting there.

Since, obviously, we aren't sitting together, I can't come through on our conversation or the pizza. But what I can do is give you a visceral demonstration of focus, by asking you to participate in the small trick—or magical experience.

Without looking up from this page, mentally create a list of all the red objects in the room. Please, stop and do this now.

Now look around you. How many red objects do you see? Before you started reading this page, your focus wasn't on red objects, so you didn't notice them. But when you focused on them, you picked out quite a few from your surroundings.

Let's go a step further. Suppose I tell you that I'll pay you $1,000 for a list of 100 red objects in the room. Talk about attention and focus! Chances are, given my (fictitious) challenge, you'd not only catalog all the obvious red objects, but you'd develop a creative streak worthy of James Joyce to flesh out the list ("If I unscrew my telephone receiver, I see red wires... If I jab my finger with this paper clip, I see red blood... If I break down my red bookcase into its components, I have six red shelves...").

How about it, small trick or magical experience? If you actually participated in the exercise, I'm sure you received a delightful jolt in discovering just how "evasive" objects are, even as they sit, unmoving, in your line of vision. This idea—of seeing what's in front of you, be it hidden ideas or objects—will run strongly through much of the work you'll do once you close this book.

In a sense, I think you'll find that *you discover what you search for, and, without your active effort in the search, an important idea or resource might as well not be there at all.*

Points to Remember

- What we focus on, in large part, determines how we lead our lives.

- Use your private writing to keep your focus on what you want out of life (sometimes, the things we find most crucial for a great life get buried under the rigors of daily existence).

  Try This: Set your timer for fifty minutes, and start it. Tell yourself about everything you currently think of as necessary for a superior life. Include material, and non-material, criteria. Make sure to take away, at least, one item from that list which you'll act upon in the next three hours.

PART FOUR

Bonus Brain Food

Bonus #1

Thought Starters

Here's a technique you're sure to put in the starting rotation. Use it when your writing seems stale, or your mind calcified.

Thought starters are fill-in questions, unlike any you encountered in school.

In school, fill-in questions were given as a way of shutting off thought; you were required to shoehorn a Correct Answer into the allotted slot before you had to hurry off to the next question.

Thought starters are open-ended fill-ins, which beg you to play, to open up your thinking rather than shut it down. Approach them as you would any private writing exercise; that is, fix the six secrets firmly in mind, set the timer, and take a header off into one. Come up for air only when the timer goes off.

- The two things I could do today to make my job more exciting would be...

- I saw a curious thing yesterday...

- I don't know much about it yet, but I'd love to learn about...

- The simplest thing I could do to make a difference would be...

- If I did the opposite of everything I normally do, my day would look like this...

- I love...

- I hate...

- I'm scared by...

- I have no explanation as to why I haven't done this yet, but I really should...

- This sounds insane, but my department would be 500% more productive if...

- This sounds inconsequential, but...

- The best part of my workday is...

- The worst part of my workday is...

- If I were guaranteed success, the project I'd take on would be...

- I'm great at _____, but I'd rather not do it because...

- I stink at _____, but I'd like to do it because...

- The three things my boss can do to help me are...

- The three things I can do to help my boss are...

- I need to brush up on...

- I should do more...

- If I went back to school now, I'd take _____, because...

- If I didn't have to work, I'd...

- I get worried when...

- If it were five years into the future, and my entire life were different, I'd live in _____, with _____, and I'd be doing...

- The two things I really want to do in my work life, but haven't yet, are...

- You know what I'd like to do again?...

- The project I'm proudest of is _____, because...

- I'd really impress myself if, starting today, I...

- I should call _____ right away, because...

- I know twenty ways to make a difference in this world, and they are...

- If I were giving a commencement speech, I'd tell the students...

Of course, you could use more than one thought starter during any bout of private writing, but I wouldn't. Let the starter direct your thinking as a beginning, but once your mind's warmed up, let it lead you where it will.

Bonus # 2

Thirteen Valuable
Writing Books

Now that extraordinary business success has been all but assured to you by virtue of your private writings, I thought you'd like to continue your writing education with a few, choice volumes. Here's a sampling of some of my favorite instructional titles, some dealing primarily with idea production, others stressing idea presentation. You'd profit, I'm sure, from picking up any one, or all, of them:

Bailey Jr., Edward P. *The Plain English Approach to Business Writing.* New York: Oxford University Press, 1997. Bailey teaches you to write simply, without dumbing down content. How does he accomplish this miracle? Through dozens of humble "suggestions," rather than the menacing, no-room-for-negotiation edicts that other advice-peddlers offer in similar books. An example of Bailey's wise advice, this one on deciding what words to use in a public document:

> "So I don't suggest you always choose the ordinary word. But—to use a word from computer terminology—make

ordinary words your default. Choose other words if precise-
ness demands, just as you do when you speak." [p. 14]

Benjamin, Susan. *Words at Work: Business Writing in Half the Time with
Twice the Power.* Massachusetts: Addison-Wesley, 1997. Benjamin
has done extensive work with corporate clients who have to get
their assignments done quickly, so this book is full of practical, re-
sults-oriented instruction. In particular, you'll want to check out
her recommendations about listing, structure, and editing.

Bradbury, Ray. *Zen in the Art of Writing: Releasing the Creative Genius
Within You.* New York: Bantam Books, 1992. If you know anything
about Bradbury, you know he loves and hates with the best of
them. In everything he writes, there seems to be an implied excla-
mation point at the end of each sentence, screaming out, "YOU
NEED TO KNOW THIS TO FULLY APPRECIATE LIFE!" As my
mom would say, "God bless him." The world needs more
Bradburys, and more books like *Zen.*

In this little book, Bradbury constantly admonishes the reader to
pick up a pencil, open a tablet, and start scribbling about something that really and truly matters.

What subject deserves such fury? Any subject, thinks Bradbury,
no matter how small, as long as it comes from a place of deep interest to you. For seventy years, Bradbury, himself, has written
about aliens, skeletons, gorillas, and sideshows—hardly pressing
subject matter for most of us. But, through his enthusiasm and
ability to tell a story, Bradbury makes us want to learn about them.

What else does Bradbury tell aspiring writers? This: "In quickness
is truth. The faster you blurt, the more swiftly you write, the more
honest you are." Ahhhh....

Dumaine, Deborah. *Write to the Top: Writing for Corporate Success*.
New York: Random House, 1989. A comprehensive writing guide
that doesn't bore or overwhelm, but instructs.

Elbow, Peter. *Writing With Power: Techniques for Mastering the Writing
Process*. New York: Oxford University Press, 1981, and *Writing
Without Teachers*. New York: Oxford University Press, 1973.
Although I've never studied with Elbow, I consider myself his dis-
ciple. Without these two books, I doubt I would have been a
writer at all. They are, quite simply, the two best books I know on
how to get at your best (and worst) thinking. They are dual bibles
on creative, continuous writing.

I, in fact, find Elbow's ideas so alluring, that I purposely stayed
away from his books while writing *Accidental Genius*. Why? I
didn't want my book to be his book—I didn't want to rip him off,
or allow his raging, forest-fire–sized notions to engulf my small,
campfire-sized ones.

Now that my book is finished, though, I slip Elbow's works off my
shelf, and page through them. On each page of each volume, it
seems, I've made some underlining or message to myself in the
margin. Among them, I've noted:

"…think for a moment about the occasions when you
spoke well. Seldom was it because you first got the beginning
just right. Usually it was a matter of a halting or even garbled
beginning, but you kept going and your speech finally became
coherent and even powerful. There is a lesson here for writing: trying to get the beginning right is a formula for failure…" [*Teachers*, p. 6]

"…there are still traces of magic left in language…What if
someone took your name and wrote it on a piece of lovely

white paper, spit on it, crumpled it up, put it in the toilet, peed on it, and then flushed it down? Names and curses, then, remind us of what was there and what can be put back if we write well." [*Power*, p. 362]

A warning: Elbow, at first blush, isn't for everyone. Because of his love of the subject, endlessly fertile mind, and ability to render his thinking onto the page, Elbow produces a lot of words, on topics that slant toward college students and teachers. No matter. For the business reader, there is still a motherload of wisdom in the non-collegiate sections of Elbow's books. Stay with them and you will be rewarded a hundred-fold.

Goldberg, Natalie. *Writing Down the Bones: Freeing the Writer Within.* Boston: Shambhala Publications, 1986. A perennial bestseller in the field of writing instruction. Goldberg packs her book with dozens of short chapters that stress the importance of writing about the "original detail" of things—such as the smell of your hallway rug, or the chip in your coffee cup. Only by paying attention to what's actually in front of you, Goldberg reasons, can you come up with prose that says something worth reading. Her other books also hold many Zen-based lessons for an ambitious reader.

Pinckert, Robert C. *Pinckert's Practical Grammar: A Lively, Unintimidating Guide to Usage, Punctuation, and Style.* Cincinnati: Writer's Digest Books, 1986. When I first read this book, I was stunned by two things: (1) It made learning grammar fun, and (2) It drove home the fact that language rules exist to help us communicate, and if you feel a certain rule isn't serving its purpose, don't use it.

Sabin, William A. *The Gregg Reference Manual.* New York: Glencoe/McGraw-Hill, 2001. Lynn Kearney, a smart writing-consult friend, considers this *the* reference book on grammar and punctuation.

Stott, Bill. *Write to the Point—And Feel Better About Your Writing*. New York: Columbia University Press. 1991. Stott, a university professor with decades of experience dealing with anxious writers, has done a remarkable job of taking daunting subjects, like "How to Find Something to Say," and breaking them down into manageable subsets.

Tarshis, Barry. *How to Write Like a Pro: A Guide to Effective Nonfiction Writing*. New York: Mentor, 1982. Remember what I said about Peter Elbow's books, that without them I wouldn't be a writer today? Well, I stand by that statement. But let me add this: without this Tarshis book, I doubt whether anyone would have wanted to read what I had written.

From studying this Tarshis book, I learned how to dress up my prose so it would hold my reader's interest. Through concepts such as "staging" and "umbrella thoughts," I discovered that my readers more clearly understood my writing if I put some space between ideas. Sounds simple, but it spells the difference between being a successful communicator, and one whose missives get chucked into the garbage.

As of this writing, *How to Write Like a Pro* is out of print. Don't let that stop you, though. Light up the Internet book search sites with your pleas for a copy. Or bug publishers to bring it back to the market. In the meantime, devour Tarshis' other excellent works. Just make sure you eventually land a copy of *Pro*.

Ueland, Barbara. *If You Want to Write: A Book about Art, Independence, and Spirit*. Saint Paul: Greywolf Press, 1987. You wouldn't think that a book originally written in 1938 by a YWCA teacher could have much application in our high-tech world of today, would you? Think again. Ueland has written a vibrant text about how we all carry genius within us naturally, and how we should abandon ourselves to the writing spirit, and damn those people who try to stop us with their "fussy-mussy" corrections. This book is low on writing rules, but high on tough-minded enthusiasm.

Once, when I interviewed former Apple computer evangelist, Guy Kawasaki, he told me that *If You Want to Write* is the best book he ever read on writing—and programming. "If you knock out the word 'writing' from the text, and stick 'programming' in its place, her ideas on that subject are just as valid," said Kawasaki.

Vitale, Joe. *CyberWriting: How to Promote Your Product or Service Online (without being flamed)*. New York: AMACOM, 1997. This is both an excellent treatise on how to write strong web copy, and how to stir up your thinking in general. Vitale adores larger-than-life people, like Mark Twain, and he writes entire chapters about the marketing lessons he's doped out from reading the work of these giants. Chapter titles include, "How Would Mark Twain Handle e-Writing?" and "The 1903 Secret for Making Millions Online." You gotta love it.

Notes

Opening Quote

Clouse, Barbara Fine. *Working it Out: A Troubleshooting Guide For Writers.* New York: McGraw-Hill, 1993. p. 17.

1 Thoughts as Currency

Elbow, Peter and Belanoff, Pat. *A Community of Writers: A Workshop Course in Writing.* New York: McGraw-Hill, 1989. p. 117.

3 Secret #1: Try Easy

Kriegel, Robert J. and Patler, Louis. *If It Ain't Broke . . . Break IT!— and Other Unconventional Wisdom for a Changing Business World.* New York: Warner Books, 1991. p. 61.

4 Secret #2: Write Fast and Continuously

Bradbury, Ray. *Zen in the Art of Writing: Releasing the Creative Genius Within You.* New York: Bantam Books, 1990. p. 13.

10 Open Up Words

Owen, Harrison. *Expanding Our Now: The Story of Open Space Technology.* San Francisco: Berrett-Koehler, 1997. pp. 69–70.

11 Get Unreal with Reality-Tweaking

Schank, Roger with Childers, Peter. *The Creative Attitude: Learning to Ask and Answer the Right Questions.* New York: MacMillan, 1988. pp. 219–221.

16 The Benefit in Growing Tired of Yourself

Whyte, David. Drawn from an interview with the author.

17 The Magic of Exact Writing

Wolfe, Tom. *The Kandy-Kolored Tangerine-Flake Streamline Baby.* Reprinted edition. New York: Bantam, Doubleday, Dell, 1999. p. xii.

Elbow, Peter. *Writing with Power: Techniques for Mastering the Writing Process.* New York: Oxford University Press, 1981. p. 236.

18 *Extract Gold from a Business Book*

Hudson, William J. *Intellectual Capital: How to Build It, Enhance It, Use It.* New York: John Wiley & Sons, 1993. p. 212.

Crosby, Philip. *The Absolutes of Leadership.* San Francisco: Jossey-Bass, 1996. p.78.

20 *You Are What You Focus On*

Bellman, Geoffrey M. *The Consultant's Calling—Bringing Who You Are to What You Do.* San Francisco: Jossey-Bass, 1990. p. 129.

Acknowledgments

While writing this book, I received spiritual and technical support from dozens of people. Here are only some of the wonderful folk who helped me:

Stella, my lovely, genius wife; Rhoda, my amazing mom; Paul, my brilliant brother (and Lynda, Craig, and Camille!); Joyce, my sensational sister; Gil Leffman, my astonishing uncle; the awesome Adelman clan; and Stella's extraordinary kin.

Karl Weber, who agented and edited this book with stunning virtuosity, while waving me around the bases; Steve Piersanti, who honored me by signing me up; Tom Peters, to whom I'll one day erect a statue for his kindness in providing the foreword; the ever-cool Berrett-Koehler staff; Alan Greenberg; Al Ries; Jay Conrad Levinson; Roger Schank; Steve "And Your Bird Can Sing" Sanderson; Paul Harris; Jon Racherbaumer; David Pogue; Cliff Hakim; David Reynolds; David Whyte; Michael Gelb; Lynn Kearney; Bob Nelson; Ray Peterson; Gates McKibben; Jay "Mincher" Matalon; Alvin "Hunya-ho" Eng; Richie and Robbie Kallman, Steve Goldberg and all my outstanding friends at Bookazine; my phenomenal bookstore pals across America; Michelle Lennox; Barry Tarshis; Geoff Bellman; Mac King; Ron Bauer; Bob Farmer; Richard Robinson; Stephen Minch; Aye Jaye; Bob Friedhoffer; Richard Wexler; Barrie Richardson; Glenn Young; Alan Robinson; Charles Manz; Ken Sweezy; Tom Fuller; Steven Varni; Ken Jedding; Jay Levin; Laura Reichert and Elizabeth Dix; Jim Autry; Chip Bell; Charles Dorris; Richard Leider; David Jamieson; Kuma and Jofu Levy; and Ray Bradbury.

Also, a special thanks to Peter Elbow for writing his books.

Index

About the Author

Mark's a salesman...who's sold over a quarter of a *billion dollars* worth of books in his career, and has been nominated three times for the prestigious *Publishers Weekly* "Sales Rep of the Year" award. He is Director of Special Projects at a large international book wholesaler.

Mark's a writer...who's written for prominent newspapers, like *The New York Times,* and publishing industry magazines. He's also served as co-creator (with David Pogue) and magic consultant on *Magic for Dummies,* which is widely considered to be the most valuable primer on magic tricks ever written.

Currently, Mark is working on another wild book of novice magic, *Mac King's Tricks with Your Head* (Crown), in which Mark and his co-author instruct readers on the finer points of (safely) jabbing a fork into their eye and pulling a drinking straw from their nose.

Visit Mark at Geniustown!

Geniustown.com is Mark's information-rich website, dedicated to teaching visitors how to tap into their own genius.

Featured on the site are...

- free articles on generating and presenting powerful money-making ideas
- excerpts from head-whacking, must-read books
- interviews with renowned achievers from a wide range of fields
- commentary from *Accidental Genius* readers on how they've used private writing in their own lives.

The site also features information about Mark's highly sought-after business seminars, workshops, and speeches on writing and thinking.